EMBRACE, EMPOWER, EDUCATE, AND INCLUDE

FOUR PRINCIPLES OF EQUITY FOR CONSCIOUS
EDUCATORS AND SCHOOLS

SALANDRA GRICE

Copyright © 2021 by Salandra Grice
Published by EduMatch®
PO Box 150324, Alexandria, VA 22315
www.edumatchpublishing.com

All rights reserved. No portion of this book may be reproduced in any form without permission from the publisher, except as permitted by U.S. copyright law. For permissions contact sarah@edumatch.org.

These books are available at special discounts when purchased in quantities of 10 or more for use as premiums, promotions fundraising, and educational use. For inquiries and details, contact the publisher: sarah@edumatch.org.

ISBN: 978-1-953852-40-3

CONTENTS

Introduction ix

1. Aiming for Equity 1
2. Embracing All Students 11
3. Empowering All Students 29
4. Educating All Students 47
5. Including All Students 79
6. All Means All 115

About the Author 121
References 123

"I am no longer accepting the things I cannot change, I am changing the things I cannot accept."
-Angela Davis

DEDICATION

For Layla and Cam. You are the reason for all that I do.

INTRODUCTION
OUT OF THE SHALLOWS

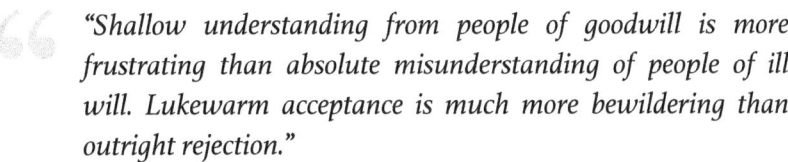

"Shallow understanding from people of goodwill is more frustrating than absolute misunderstanding of people of ill will. Lukewarm acceptance is much more bewildering than outright rejection."

— Dr. Martin Luther King, Jr., *Letter from a Birmingham Jail*
(1963)

Think for a moment about the following statement: *The continued presence of the racial achievement gap is not merely an indication of how poorly individual students perform, but more of an indication of a school's lack of effectiveness to teach certain students.* Is this statement true or false? How one answers the previous question depends on one's understanding of the importance of culturally responsive and equity-based practices in the classroom. As education statistics continue to point to areas in need of improvement (National Center for Education Statistics (NCES), 2017b), effective culturally responsive and equity-minded educators are critical to the reform of educational opportunities, outcomes, and experiences for marginalized students in the classroom (Banks, 2019; Gay, 2010; Gorski, 2019; Ladson-Billings, 2009). Unfortunately, many culturally responsive and equity-based efforts fall short of meeting the needs of diverse students because many educators and school institutions have not had practice in developing sound, in-depth principles of culturally responsive or equity-based teaching practices (Gorski, 2016a, 2016b, 2019).

In today's educational landscape of increased efforts and attention towards diversity, equity, inclusion, cultural responsiveness, and (more recently) anti-racism and Critical Race Theory, many educators have shallow understandings (or flat-out rejections) of many of these approaches. Many are stuck in the comforts of tradition and convention and hold tightly to "the way things are," finding it difficult to break the chains of conformity to see that changes are needed and necessary. These same teachers and schools claim to value equity and want to do what's best for all students; yet, they shutter, resist, and turn away when they encounter approaches that prove to be more effective yet are nontraditional in meeting those needs. We can't claim to want to see different results if we are unwilling to do anything different to make it happen. Teachers must get real about the equity efforts in education and become truly responsive educators by getting out of the shallows, diving deeper, and getting real about what it takes to become an effective educator for *every* culturally, linguistically, socioeconomically, differently-abled, and religiously diverse student.

In my first book, *The Conscious Educator: Becoming Culturally Responsive Teachers and Schools* (2019, 2020), I highlighted the path to helping teachers develop the mindset in order to become better equipped to meet the needs of their diverse students. This work's goal was to point teachers in the direction to begin their journey in becoming a *conscious educator*. A conscious educator is committed to being a change agent in the classroom, knows and understands their students, and uses the most effective practices to help reach and teach every student, every day. Becoming a conscious educator is the only way for educators to embody the characteristics of a culturally responsive and equity-focused teacher.

In their purest forms, "culturally responsive teaching involves using the cultures, experiences, and perspectives of African, Native, Latino and Asian American students as filters through which to teach them academic knowledge and skills" (Gay & Kirkland, 2003, p.181). It also involves, but is not limited to, "...unpacking unequal distributions of power and privilege, and teaching students of color cultural competence about themselves and each other." (Gay & Kirkland, 2003, p. 181). I would even expand this definition to include that ALL students deserve to see themselves and others in a more accurate and complete light. Every student hails from a diverse background and should be able to learn about differences through positive representations of themselves and others.

While equity in education means ensuring all students have the unique supports they need to flourish and thrive, an equity-focused pedagogy is "teaching strategies and classroom environments that help students from diverse racial, ethnic, and cultural groups attain the knowledge, skills, and attitudes needed to function effectively within, and help create and perpetuate, a just, humane, and democratic society" (Banks & Banks, 1995, p. 152). Although having different entry points, both approaches ultimately aim for the same goal: providing access and opportunity for all students to reach academic, social, emotional, and economic success in school and society. Both approaches seek to accomplish this by focusing on fairness, justice, and equity in education. Both seek to disrupt the status quo of inequity by creating equitable spaces for all students. With all that equity-based practices have to offer, it should be easy for all teachers, administrators, and educational stakeholders to get on board and begin teaching through a lens of equity and cultural responsiveness. Sadly, this assumption is far from reality.

It may feel like the recent surge of attention surrounding equity efforts is an indication that culturally responsive teaching and equity-based practices are now commonplace, openly accepted, and implemented on all campuses by educators at large. Unfortunately, for many classrooms and schools across the country, culturally responsive teaching and equity-based practices are not yet the norm. Many marginalized students attend schools and reside in classrooms with teachers who are not effective in culturally responsive practices and have even less understanding of equity issues (Gorski, 2016b). As a result, it is common for many students of color, many English language learners, students with special needs, LGBTQIA+ students, and many students living at and below the poverty line to experience learning environments that are not only unresponsive, but they are also negative, discriminatory, and academically unengaging (Milner et al., 2019). Education research confirms this as it says these students are routinely sent to the office more often for subjective infractions (Milner et al., 2019); they receive suspensions at higher rates for the same offenses as their White counterparts (Howard, 2016); have higher and more violent interactions with school resources officers (Milner et al., 2019); and receive harsher punishments (Wilson & Yull, 2018). At the same time, they also receive less than engaging curriculum (Hammond, 2015; Loewen, 2007) and are often exposed to lower expectations and deficit beliefs about their abilities and potentials on behalf of their teachers than their White counterparts (Valencia, 2010). These disparities are long-standing, but not immovable. The solution to overturning many of these negative statistics lies in our commitment to pursuing cultural responsiveness and equity in every aspect of our educational environments.

Unfortunately, many of our stated commitments to equity and cultural responsiveness have only been reflected in mission statements on school websites, marquees, and newsletters. Many schools have not sought to make the tangible changes necessary to disrupt inequity and reproduce the cultural responsiveness they proclaim to value. Many schools stay stuck in inequity ruts because they are still focused and satisfied with simple, surface-level, cultural or diversity celebrations, and equality initiatives. Let's start with the problem of culture as a celebration first.

The Pitfalls of the Culture Craze

For many campuses across the country, cultural crafts, pot lucks, multicultural festivals, and other one-dimensional activities are the extent of their commitments to culturally responsive efforts. Yes, multicultural festivals and celebrations are important in manifesting more culturally responsive environments; however, they should not be the end of those efforts. These common displays of "culture fetish" (Gorski, 2016b, p. 222) and calls for racial harmony can often undermine the intended purpose of authentic culturally responsive efforts. Too many educators are finding comfort and complacency in simple focuses on cultural artifacts such as foods, clothing, and festivals as these non-threatening consumptions of culture provided a shield for them away from the more uncomfortable complexities of cultural differences in the form of experiences with historical oppression, racism, discrimination, and marginalization that occurs between cultural groups. More than just a nod to diversity and tolerance for close proximity to people of color, cultural responsiveness should seek to elevate the histories, perspectives, values, and beliefs of historically (and currently) marginalized groups (Torres, 2019). It should also seek to upend the default adherence to, prioritization of, and forced assimilation to White cultural norms, values, and beliefs in schools and elevate the norms, values, and beliefs of historically marginalized student groups to an equitable status. When this is not understood, schools with good intentions still miss the mark as the racism, sexism, homophobia, ableism, religious bigotry, and classism students face remains unaddressed. It is ineffective to allow students to bring in a favorite dish from home if the home language they speak is deemed inappropriate or not "proper" English for the school setting. It is pointless to allow students to produce hip-hop operas or participate in "cyphers" (Emdin, 2016) if the unjust experiences they face in the world (and in schools) in the form of police brutality and economic injustice are deemed inappropriate or "too political" for the school environment. Such is not a culturally responsive environment if it is unresponsive and hostile to students' culture and everyday experiences.

Equity vs. Equality

The same can be said for their equity and equality efforts too. Most are too focused on equality and never fully reach the ultimate goal of equity as a foundational starting point. Though equality, or providing all students with the same resources, is a good start, it should not signal the end of our equity efforts. Assessing whether or not all students have equal access to resources, high-quality curricula, qualified teachers, and fair treatment is only the starting point of creating an equitable learning environment. Educational policymakers should be focused on ensuring that all school facilities are equal in that they are all safe, all well-funded, and all committed to providing a quality education to all students. However, to obtain those fair, just, and commonsense conditions, an equity approach is required. An equity approach recognizes that although all students should have the same things, they are not all in the same position to receive them and may need different amounts of those resources to help them succeed. As the famous equity sketch depicts three students standing in front of a fence trying to view a baseball game demonstrates, equality is not equity.

Image source: https://oneworldgifted.weebly.com/blog/why-i-hate-the-equality-vs-equity-graphic

In the illustration, each student has a different obstacle keeping them from viewing the baseball game, and they are all given the same support in the name of equality to solve their problem. As a result, giving each student the same (or equal) resource, such as a crate in order to see, doesn't quite cut it. The taller student now has an even further advantage; the middle student has a better view, but still not as good as the taller student. The shorter student, even though he is given the same crate, still cannot see the game. The last student (illustrating the failure of equality efforts), still wanting the same opportunity to see the game, still couldn't because the crate was not enough. He needed something different to meet his needs.

However, this famous depiction was notably critiqued as flawed as well. In its attempts to illustrate how to level the playing field or give each student an equitable chance to see the game, it assumes a deficit in two of the students by making them shorter. It misses the opportunity to truly be fair in its approach as the barrier (the fence) was never removed. If we assume the problem is with the student and we never remove the fence, we cannot insist that the situation is equitable. Seeing students and their families as whole humans and removing barriers that limit opportunities is what equity and cultural responsiveness are all about. We become equitable when we remove the barrier of tracking which pre-determines what levels of learning students are capable of (Johnson, 2019). We become culturally responsive when we remove the barrier of arbitrary dress codes which punish students of color for their culturally affirming hairstyles (Lattimore, 2017). We become both culturally responsive and equitable when the curriculum reflects the experiences, perspectives, and contributions of many diverse groups, not just those that mainstream, White, middle-class norms have socialized many to believe to be more acceptable (Ladson-Billings, 2009). If we are not ready to remove these barriers, how can we say we are really committed to equity in our schools?

Getting Below the Surface

The remedy to this dilemma involves ensuring educators and schools move deeper and more authentically into equity practices. Some key components in teachers being able to embody these practices in the classroom relies on them having ample opportunity to self-reflect on current beliefs about inequity, be able to recognize and redress inequities, and finally be able to implement fair, just, and equitable practices in its place (Gorski, 2016b; Grice, 2019). Whitewashing education ignores many of the structural and institutional inequalities present within our schools. Schools can no longer claim to be culturally responsive or equity-focused if they have yet to understand the needs of their diverse students and address the approaches and practices that have caused the marginalization of these students and families. To put it plainly, if your school's understanding of equity ignores the racism, sexism, homophobia, transphobia, classism, and ableism students contend with every day, your school is not committed to eradicating inequity; you are committed to maintaining it (Banks & Banks, 1995). Ultimately, the path toward equity in schools "begins with the willingness to see what we might be conditioned not to see. It begins with the humility to consider our and our colleagues' culpability" in reproducing inequities (Gorski, 2016a). Let's open our eyes to the possibilities of this new vision. Let's be teachers who can see inequity, address it, and eradicate it.

This vision to move educators towards a deeper equity commitment came about after years of witnessing and experiencing various forms of this phenomenon as a student, novice educator, and parent. My first book, *The Conscious Educator: Becoming Culturally Responsive Teachers and Schools,* provided a firm foundation to aid teachers during their journey in becoming culturally conscious educators. However, the journey doesn't stop with cultural knowledge, cultural competency, or cultural awareness; it only begins it. This book will take educators to the next level in becoming a conscious educator by giving strategies and guidance in keeping schools on target in their culturally responsive goals while aiming for the end result: equity in schools.

In my pursuit of working with educators and administrators on deepening their understanding of culturally responsive teaching and equity-based practices, I have found four guiding principles to be effective in helping them become truly responsive and equity-focused advocates. The following four principles outlined throughout the rest of this book will help educators create positive and equitable school environments which: *embrace* and affirm the diversity of the students in their care; *empower* students to create positive change in their world; *educate* students with critical and academically challenging curricula; and *include* historically marginalized voices, perspectives, and experiences to make learning more relevant, engaging, meaningful, and equitable for ALL students. Are you ready for the next part of the journey?

Let's continue...

1. AIMING FOR EQUITY

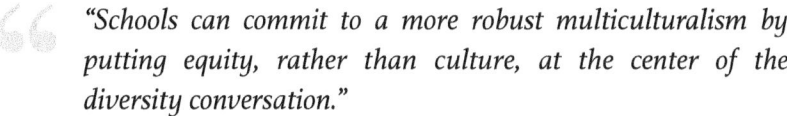
"Schools can commit to a more robust multiculturalism by putting equity, rather than culture, at the center of the diversity conversation."

— Paul C. Gorski & Katy Swalwell, *Equity Literacy for All*

In a more perfect world, there would be significant progress in culturally responsive teaching and equity among schools. One could celebrate an increase in competent educators who were fully engaged and confident in their culturally responsive and equity-focused practices. Ideally, stories about students of color and their near-perfect and positive experiences at school at the hands of truly culturally responsive educators would be regular conversation. It would be exciting to share that students are in a school with narrowing racial achievement gaps, declining discipline rates, and equitable funding. It would be great to share how they feel a sense of inclusion, care, and safety, and are taught with rigorous curricula in positive and culturally affirming ways. It would be monumental to share that this is all being done by multiethnic, multilingual, equity-minded teachers, teacher-aides, and administrators. But I don't have a story like that today. However, stories about schools who are meeting these criteria and excelling in an equitable environment do exist. That's why there is such a need for more culturally responsive and equity-based practices to reach larger audiences so that the academic, behavioral, and social benefits can be far-reaching (Banks; 2019; Gay, 2010; Hammond, 2015). Unfortunately, today is not that day.

Let's begin with the story of an African American girl who suffered from sleep apnea and was taking medication to correct the disorder. Sometimes, like most of us, she got a little cranky when she didn't get enough sleep. Although her teachers knew of her medical condition, her tantrums were too much for the teachers and administrators in charge of her care to endure, and they decided to call the police during this episode. She was arrested, handcuffed, and taken to a police station to be fingerprinted (Bowden, 2019). This little girl was only six-years-old.

Another story takes place in Idaho, where teachers dressed up as stereotypical Mexican Americans and created a "Make America Great Again" (MAGA) wall during a celebration for their "respect" character trait (Rosenberg, 2018). These teachers promptly apologized for their actions and felt they had no "malicious intent" regarding their actions. However, I wonder what intent the Latino students who attended their school received, especially in the wake of today's heavily contested immigration policies and practices. And finally, I have to remind you of the story of an African American boy who I discussed in my first book, David. When he was unwilling to stand in line in the cafeteria "properly," he was denied the opportunity to eat breakfast and sent to class to begin his day crying and on an empty stomach. He was only 5-years-old.

These experiences are quite common for many marginalized students. Instances of hate, indifference, neglect, inhumane treatment, and otherwise cultural incompetence are common experiences for many students of color, many English language learners, students with special needs, and many students living below the poverty line as they disproportionately have negative experiences such as these at the hands of educators (Milner et al., 2019). Experiences like this are unfortunate for these students and my former student David. Although the teachers in the stories may have felt no ill-intent, may have even had the culturally responsive and diversity trainings, received the checklists on equity, even brushed up on their Black or Hispanic Heritage Month facts, or hosted a multicultural fair after school, many are not yet the culturally responsive nor equity-minded educators they claim to be. They are not yet effective in overturning many of the negative statistics for marginalized students because they are stuck on the shallow end of the pool of culturally responsive and equity-based practices. We've got to go deeper.

Equity *IS* Possible

Although equity issues are not new and education scholars have been screaming from the hilltops for decades about what needs to be done to improve the educational opportunities for all students (Banks, 2019; Gay, 2010; Ladson-Billings, 2009), many of those pleas have often fallen on deaf ears. Teachers, bogged down by bureaucratic demands, have not had the time nor energy to put another educational initiative on their plate. As a result, equity initiatives have been last on many school agendas. From naysayers proclaiming that equity is not possible for a number of financial and political reasons, to others' explicit efforts to undermine any gains in equity progress (Walters, 2020), the COVID-19 pandemic revealed how far we still have to go in meeting the needs of all students, but more importantly, that doing so *is* possible.

When the seriousness of the COVID-19 virus became apparent across the nation, immediate measures were put in place to ensure the spread of this virus was slowed to a sustainable halt (Center for Disease Control, 2020). One of the most drastic (and necessary) measures implemented was the closure of the majority of the U.S.'s PreK-12 educational institutions (Wendlandt, 2020). These closures would keep many students out of school for several months. This measure meant that many students would be at home with no formal instruction for an extended period of time. The scramble to keep kids "on track" sparked a call for virtual learning measures to be implemented as a solution (Li & Lalani, 2020). Among the most pressing issues during a time of job losses, childcare issues, health concerns, and access to toilet paper, many families did not have a computer at home, and many more did not have access to high-quality internet (Hirsch, 2020). Lack of access to technology for many families was not new and has been an issue for some time (Ed Trust-West, 2020). Just like these long-standing technology concerns, issues of equity came back screaming; this time, it was front and center. This time, it could no longer be ignored.

In response, many efforts were enacted to help families in need during this unprecedented interruption in their everyday lives (USA.-GOV, 2020). School districts gave out food to families, and many virtual educational providers also gave free subscriptions to their online services (Lascala, 2020). This may all seem like common sense responses during an international disaster; unfortunately, we can't forget the traumatic political environment the U.S. was currently in where words like "socialism" were being used as a scare tactic to shame people who advocated for presidential candidates whose platforms were grounded in equity efforts in the form of safety-nets for its citizens (Hobson & Hagan, 2020). It was amazing to see how what was said couldn't be done and shouldn't be done (i.e., un-American) was now being handed down in droves by naysayers just a week later. This change of heart led me to believe that not only was equity possible, but it was simply a matter of will. For our schools, if we want equity to become common-place in the minds and hearts of those in the position to implement it, we've got to start aiming for it more ferociously. It can no longer just be a mission statement; it has to be *the* mission. Educational stakeholders, educators, and students have to believe in the power of equity and be committed to its implementation. In order to create true equity in our schools, we have to be knowledgeable of the needs of our students and be ready to do the work to provide it. We've got to come together for the greater good of all students.

Equity Detours

Even when our schools' commitments to equity have become the priority, many equity initiatives and efforts across many schools are controlled and managed by those least invested in seeing it come to fruition (Gorski, 2019). Developing equity-minded teachers and schools becomes impossible when efforts to do so are subjugated to mainstream calls for comfort in all aspects of professional development. Equity initiatives are not about being comfortable; it's about straining towards equity in spite of the discomfort. Many of the discomforts involved in eradicating inequities in schools can be a deterrent for those accustomed to maintaining norms of deference and compliance in all school matters. The "calling out" of the discriminatory and oppressive school practices many of us are accustomed to can trigger many educators' dedication to maintain tradition at all costs. Defensiveness, denial, anger, and guilt are only a few of the common emotional detours equity work can take educators through. Some of these detours can alter the path to equity efforts before educators have a chance to make any positive changes. As equity topics revolve around discussions of race, ethnicity, class, gender, and sexual orientation, teachers must be prepared to push through their discomfort and increase their stamina during these difficult dialogues (DiAngelo, 2018).

In Paul Gorski's 2019 article entitled "Avoiding Racial Equity Detours," he highlights four common *equity detours* that keep schools from authentically embracing equity initiatives. These detours include the roadblocks of *pacing for privilege, poverty of culture, deficit ideology,* and *celebrating diversity*. When *pacing for privilege*, equity efforts and initiatives are often paced for those with the least amount of investment in equity matters while at the same time punishing those with the most. Too often, those with the least amount of comfort, tolerance, or experience in discussing educational inequalities run the show, and those whose equity visions are more clearly defined and action-oriented are labeled as "angry" or "aggressive" (especially Black educators). In this detour, the politics and White cultural norms of "niceness" supersede the efforts to create conditions that are actually conducive for students and families because some feel uncomfortable in participating in the necessary dialogues and actions needed to do so.

The *poverty of culture* combined with *deficit ideology* sidetrack equity efforts as they rest in deficit perceptions of students, their family, culture, and background while using these assumptions to blame them for the academic difficulties they may experience. They say students continue to suffer from academic and discipline disparities because they inherently lack something necessary to help them succeed. This mindset says that Black students are suspended at higher rates than any other student group because they are worst-behaved, not because of racial bias among educators. It says that Black, Latinx, and Native American students perform lower on standardized tests because they don't care about education or are unintelligent, not because they are subject to lower quality curricula, under-qualified teachers, and fewer resources than schools with majority White students (Gay, 2010). The inherent lack of accountability these roadblocks create ensures educators who are distracted by them are constantly caught up in a blame-game between students, parents, and their families instead of operating from a shared accountability lens that allows for the redressing of these educational issues, not the passing on of them to others.

Finally, the *celebrating diversity* detour is a detour many schools remain stuck within. Many schools have very good intentions to make sure all students feel welcomed and included. Unfortunately, these efforts are only on the surface and are limited in depth, and lack a real exploration of students' lives and cultural experiences. A blind eye is continuously turned to the academic and discipline racial disparities on many campuses, and all energy is focused on highlighting how happy schools are to have "diversity" in the building while pointing to posters and inspirational quotes from people of color on the walls. Visual representation of diverse people in our schools is important, but don't let these detours derail your campus from making more meaningful, authentic, and impactful gains towards equity, too.

Gorski (2019) reminds educators that we don't have to fall victim to these detours if we stay focused on what he calls *equity literacy* principles. Instead of avoiding discomfort in discussions of racism, sexism, classism, ableism, or homophobia, he recommends we directly confront manifestations of these isms in our schools. Instead of focusing on "fixing" what is perceived to be wrong with marginalized students, he says to examine the policies and practices in your school that block access to opportunity and learning for these students. Instead of assuming a school's superiority in knowing what's best for students, we must center students' and their family's voices so that they can speak to *us* about what *they* need. However, evidence surrounding common school practices and policies indicates many schools are still too focused on their needs instead of the needs of their students and families.

From School-Centric to Student/Family-Centered

Many schools operate from a well-intentioned viewpoint; educational professionals believe they always "know what's best" for the students and families they serve. After all, they are professionals, have obtained all the degrees, and have years of experience in teaching and education. In this view of educators being the all-knowing holders of the knowledge of what is best for students, a lens that recognizes the historically oppressive practices instituted by public schools throughout the history of the U.S. becomes critical in addressing the flaws of the assumed superiority of institutional knowledge and practice.

Many scholars have pointed out in great detail the many oppressive, discriminatory, and racist policies found within the practices of many schools (e.g., Hoffman, 2014; Johnson, 2019). Historically, public schools have been institutions meant to socialize and assimilate marginalized groups into the norms of the dominant White, middle-class norms and create a compliant workforce for businesses and corporations (Adams, 1995; Anderson, 1988; Johnson, 2019). The methods used and ideologies pushed to accomplish these aims have been the basis of many of the injustices marginalized people continue to suffer from today.

Native American and Indigenous groups can attest to the harm in family separations; their children were stolen and shipped off to American and Canadian boarding schools to "civilize" them into White culture (Adams, 1995; Carlisle Indian School Project, 2020). African American, Latinx, and Asian/Pacific Islander families can attest to the centuries-long fight for the right to participate in daily activities like pursuing an education (Anderson, 1999; Blanton, 2007; Kaur, 2018; Tamura, 1993). Many of these groups have firsthand experience of how their dreams for education to be the gateway of freedom turned into the pits of subordination, colonization, and erasure at the hands of the institutions proclaiming to "know what's best" for them and their families. Building trust between marginalized communities and schools continues to be a struggle because of this history. The solution requires an adjustment in how schools approach the families they serve. Instead of continuing to force the "Americanized" agenda onto students and families, a commitment to create more equitable collaborations which includes the needs of both the families and schools needs to be established (Ishimaru, 2020). Education scholar Ann M. Ishimaru (2020) highlights the kind of mind shift needed to make these changes when she states:

> Our educational systems contain both historically rooted dynamics of oppression and possibilities for just futures and collective well-being. Change requires both disrupting what's already in motion and figuring out which practices, policies, and systems should replace the status quo. Both families and educators have expertise we need in order to "fix" our systems---and both need to build capacity to work toward systemic change (pp. 140-141).

Are schools ready for the shift from school-centric norms in which educational institutions continue to require attendance in school-based meetings and activities that focus on "fixing" families? Are they ready to see the students and families they serve as partners in education? Are they open to hearing their knowledge and insights to help make schools truly responsive and equitable for all students? If they are, a plan of action to take them to the equity promised land is the next step.

Four Principles for Greater Equity in Schools

While the promises of equity still remain to be seen for many campuses, we don't have to continue "waiting for Superman" (YouTube Movies, 2012) to begin walking down the path towards increased equity and access to opportunity for our students. Because the path to equity is paved with decades of educational research, it can be overwhelming to attack each theory and practice from so many different sources and viewpoints. To help educators synthesize and actualize the main goals of equity work in schools, the remainder of this book will focus on four principles that help teachers and schools work toward equity. These principles, if used appropriately, will help educators and schools create the positive changes they seek for their students and stay committed to culturally responsive and equity-based practices. By no means are the components of these four principles exhaustive nor a one-and-done method to creating equitable schools. This is only a framework to help educators manage the complex and multifaceted work of creating equity in their schools and focus their efforts on key components. These principles, which glean from the work of scholars such as James A. Banks, Geneva Gay, Gloria Ladson-Billings, Paul Gorski, Sonia Nieto, Christine Sleeter, and many more, will help educators make sense of equity initiatives and become better equipped to evaluate their own practices to ensure they are accurately aiming for equity as well.

On the next page, you will find **Figure 1**, which illustrates the principles and components involved. The rest of this book will elaborate on each principle's practices and approaches, along with steps to guide implementation in classrooms and schools. Suggestions will be made to help educators apply these principles in their teaching, help students and families become included in the processes, and encourage school leaders to hold themselves and their campuses accountable to these measures.

Embrace
Provide a welcoming and affirming environment.

Develop authentic and caring relationships with students and families.

Engage in the reduction and elimination of racist, discriminatory, or oppressive policies and practices.

Empower
Develop collaborative partnerships with parents, families, and the community.

Develop a sense of agency in students to make positive changes in their world and challenge the inequities they see.

Create an empowering school culture.

Educate
Utilize culturally relevant curricula and resources.

Create equitable learning environments where all students can learn using their strengths.

Teachers and students are co-collaborators in knowledge.

Foster high expectations for every student.

Include
Utilize teaching materials that provide windows and mirrors into the lives of diverse peoples.

Include multiple perspectives in constructing knowledge and welcome the use of diverse learning styles.

Create inclusive school policies that allow students to stay connected to the school community.

Figure 1. Four Principles for Equity-Focused Classrooms and Schools

Questions for Reflection

1. What is your understanding of equity and equality? How does it differ from the explanation in the chapter?
2. Does your campus currently use any approaches to address issues of inequity? If not, why?
3. How effective are your campus's current efforts to address inequities?
4. Have you noticed any of the equity detours discussed being a hindrance in your school's equity efforts? How will you seek to avoid these detours in the future?

2. EMBRACING ALL STUDENTS

> *"Our task must be to free ourselves... by widening our circle of compassion to embrace all living creatures and the whole of nature and its beauty."*
>
> — ALBERT EINSTEIN

Multicultural education pioneer James A. Banks (2019) profoundly clarifies the importance of understanding culture when he states, "individuals who know the world only from their own cultural perspectives are denied important parts of the human experience and are culturally and ethnically encapsulated" (p. 2). In becoming a conscious educator, it is especially important to understand one's own culture and positionality, as well as the culture of diverse students and their families.

In understanding positionality, it is important for educators to examine the many dynamics which have influenced them throughout their lives. Many of our beliefs, values, and attitudes have been shaped as a result of the experiences and people we have encountered. It is also important to note the intersecting identities we all carry, which also inform thoughts, actions, and beliefs in matters of the world and in education. If we viewed the world through the lens in which *we* see, how effective would we be for the students and families we serve if we do not understand their intersecting identities and their lens as well?

Every student deserves a learning environment that is welcoming and affirming of the many identities they bring into the classroom. This kind of environment works to ensure that every student is acknowledged as essential and relevant to the learning process. This environment embraces all students and makes them feel safe and valued, and included. It is also a foundational aspect of building a positive and caring school climate. To do this, we must know more about student likes, dislikes, learning styles, family background, learning preferences, favorite books, and even communication patterns, and be accepting of them. Even more so, we must have authentic knowledge about their cultures and identities. Essentially, teachers must begin to reconcile with the warnings from multicultural scholars such as Dr. James A. Banks (2019), Dr. Geneva Gay (2010), and Dr. Gloria Ladson-Billings (2009) as they all make it explicitly clear: culture is central to learning. Teachers who ignore or are hostile towards the culture and identities of the students in their care are essentially ignoring important components that create meaningful and engaging learning environments (Gay, 2010). Teachers must understand that transforming the educational opportunities and outcomes for our diverse students "requires that they have knowledge of the cultural characteristics of different ethnic groups and of how culture affects teaching and learning" (Gay, 2010, p. 245). This understanding helps to implement the first component of embracing all students and creating more equitable classrooms. In doing so, we must stop and ask ourselves: Are our schools places where all students feel they belong?

Providing a Welcoming and Affirming Environment

"Belongingness is an essential human need and motivation" (Finley, 2018, p. 37). The need to belong is so powerful that Maslow (1970) lists it in his Hierarchy of Needs. Most people need to feel connected to one another and so do our students. Educational researchers have been helping make these connections for us for quite some time (Goodenow, 1993); however, the need to make sure students' social and emotional health is also considered has only begun trending recently (Weissberg, 2016). Nonetheless, "students' sense of being accepted, valued, included, and encouraged by others (teacher and peers) in the academic classroom setting and of feeling oneself to be an important part of the life and activity of the class" is essential to creating welcoming and affirming classrooms and schools (Goodenow, 1993, p. 25). When this need is not met, students can experience a lack of motivation, anxiety, depression, loneliness, and isolation, which can lead to increases in bullying and suicide (Beck & Malley, 2003; Kunc, 1992; Santhanam, 2019; Slaten et al., 2014; Zhou & Zhang, 2014). Teachers can help interrupt these experiences by increasing their understanding of the many ways in which schools traditionally marginalize, exclude, and erase the identities of students from nondominant and otherwise diverse backgrounds and replace those practices with more equitable efforts to affirm those student identities.

To do this, a basic understanding of the roles that dominant and nondominant identities play in the school environment is essential (Grice, 2019/2020). In a racialized society such as the U.S., centuries of colonization, subordination, cultural genocide, and discrimination have created a complex power structure where those among the "dominant" groups are provided greater access to opportunity than those among the "nondominant" (Tatum, 1997). In the U.S., historically marginalized and therefore nondominant groups (in terms of structural and institutionalized power) have been people of color, women, immigrants, lower-income, homeless, LGBTQIA+, non-Christian religious, the disabled, and English language learners, among others (Takaki, 2008; Zinn, 2003). On the other hand, the dominant group (in terms of structural and institutionalized power) identify as White, middle and upper class, male, cis-gender, English-speaking, non-disabled, and Christian (Koppelman, 2017). These dynamics have been in play since the signing of the U.S. Constitution in 1787, and (as it was intended) sources of power and greater access to opportunity have been limited to a few (Kendi, 2016). The slow work of overturning the status quo has been long and hard, but history has proven that justice can prevail. Yes, Dr. King's words ring true today more than ever—*the arc of time does bend towards justice, and the time for educational justice is now!*

Regardless of its importance, taking readers on a tour of historical oppression in the U.S. inflicted on nondominant groups is not the ultimate goal in this discussion. However, a glance at the works of professor Ibram X. Kendi's *Stamped from the Beginning* (2016), Michelle Alexander's *The New Jim Crow* (2012), Edward E. Baptist's *The Half Has Never Been Told* (2014), Dee Brown's *Bury My Heart at Wounded Knee* (1970), James Anderson's *The Education of Blacks in the South, 1860-1935 (1988)*, or Ronald Takaki's *Strangers from Different Shore* (1998) will give educators a firm foundation in the truth about America's dark founding principles and help them make significant connections to how the legacy of oppression continues to harm communities today. These legacies, which have infected every aspect of American life, can also be seen in our schools.

Just as dominant identities have been favored throughout society, they have also been held in high esteem in our schools. As teacher demographics continue to remain White, female, and middle-class, the preferred and reinforced social and cultural norms in our schools reflect similar findings (Miller, 2018). As a result, experiences of marginalized groups are often white-washed, minimized, or erased in many classrooms and schools. Nondominant students are often forced to assimilate into the mainstream White cultural expectations of their schools or risk failure, exclusion, or harsh disciplinary action as a result (Tran & Birman, 2017). Teachers, it's time for this practice to end. It's time for all students to feel fully included and accepted in their school and to see themselves equitably represented in their school environment and treated as worthy.

To evaluate whose identities are valued and positively affirmed on your campus, teachers can first take an overall assessment of the physical environment of their classroom or school. In this assessment, teachers should look to see whether or not there is a variety of cultures, ethnicities, and languages represented in their classroom and school

(Derman-Sparks, 1989). If teachers notice an overrepresentation of dominant images and norms that relate to one specific culture or race while lacking representation of other cultures and races of students, this is an opportunity to create more inclusive changes. Take this opportunity to begin promoting a diverse variety of people, cultures, experiences, socioeconomic statuses, sexual orientations, abilities, ages, religions, and languages for the benefit of all students. Display quotes, books, pictures, or artwork from a variety of cultural groups, not just during special heritage months, but throughout the year. This small act of simply providing representation of diverse people in school decor can go a long way in sending a message about what you value and *who* you value. But it shouldn't stop with posters and pictures.

Ultimately, creating a space where all students and families feel welcome also means showing them *they* are welcome, too. The inclusion of voices and experiences of nondominant groups has been missing in many school improvement plans. Too often, the needs of diverse students and families go unmet because no one has asked them what they need (Khalifa, 2018). Start asking! Distribute parent, student, or family surveys at the beginning of the year to see what families need, what their concerns are, and what they can offer to help schools create positive environments for every student. Don't let these surveys be superficial gestures. Utilize the knowledge and suggestions of parents and ask them to help you implement them. Creating parent/teacher collaborations where all voices are valued can go a long way in helping create an atmosphere where all members of the school community feel they matter.

Creating school environments where all students and families feel included is essential to any progress in school equity initiatives. Learning environments where all cultures and identities are embraced and have a sense of belonging will make greater progress towards equity than those with hostile or negative school environments. This simple act of not only acknowledging and ensuring all persons are valued will make embracing students by building caring and authentic relationships an easier process.

Developing Authentic and Caring Relationships with Students and Families

Relationships matter. Relationships matter so much that no successful collaboration between people can happen unless they have a positive and trusting rapport or bond. Think about some of music's all-time famous groups. Across all music styles and genres, from the Temptations to the Beatles to New Edition and even Destiny's Child, good music is made when there are good relationships between the musicians. Any episode of VH1's *Behind the Music* or TV One's *Unsung* can demonstrate that once those relationships diminish, so does the music. As educators, we are trying to make music with our students in the form of creating academic and social success in and beyond the classroom. If our relationships with our students are sour, tainted, or never fully develop, how do we expect to create experiences of school success? We can't.

Positive relationships between teachers and students are critical to the learning process (Meador, 2019). Positive teacher-student relationships are so critical that they affect students not only academically but socially as well. These relationships, when fostered correctly, provide students with a sense of relatedness, security, and the safety needed to tackle challenging academic learning tasks essential for higher-order and critical thinking abilities (Birch & Ladd, 1997; Cassetta & Sawyer, 2015). It is critical that these relationships start as soon as students enter school. Research has found that students who have more positive social relationships with their elementary teachers also have more positive social relationships with their secondary teachers as well (Cassetta & Sawyer, 2015). Unfortunately, not every student has the opportunity to build these kinds of relationships with their teachers. I am reminded of a former student I inherited from another teacher that was having difficulty supporting a caring environment for him to illustrate my point.

Esteban joined my class after he had turned over and thrown one too many chairs in his previous kindergarten class. However, this little boy was not having trouble academically, only behaviorally. Even though I had heard the horror stories from his previous teacher about his behaviors, he got a clean slate when he came to my classroom. When he did attempt to test the waters (as many children do), he was promptly reminded of the positive expectations I had of him, and I promptly praised him once he complied. After a few weeks of this pattern, it was established that Esteban was never going to be the "perfect" student, but he responded to the "warm demander" tone in my classroom, and he aimed to please. He was a brilliant boy who loved to learn and had many interests. While having him in my class, I realized that he was also a very sensitive boy who loathed being wrong. He disdained it so much that it was one of the triggers that would set off aggressive and noncompliant behaviors in the classroom. I sought to minimize this by lessening the competitiveness of the games we played. I kept a cool head and tone in my classroom during his meltdowns. By the end of the year, many of my students were mimicking my behaviors as I would hear them say to each other, "just go with the flow," when someone seemed on the verge of a meltdown. One of the things that I also found helpful in creating a more caring environment as a primary school teacher was to get rid of my behavior chart. I no longer kept tabs on inappropriate behaviors. I just praised and encouraged them to increase behaviors I wanted to see. They didn't disappoint, even Esteban.

This simple act of rebelling against tradition by getting rid of the behavior chart released students of the constant reminder (and reminding their friends) that they had done something "bad." It was all we needed to maintain a positive and caring classroom environment where students felt free to make mistakes, but were also encouraged to try again to do better. In place of keeping track of mistakes on a behavior chart, I created a system of collecting points for a job well done. Although I was still constrained and tied to maintaining the behavioral contracts set forth by my campus, I did my best to make it work in favor of my students. Every student was able to earn something, no one had what they had earned taken away, and I was able to remind students of the progress they were making and encourage them to continue to do their best.

The often-negative relationships that children from nondominant groups experience with their teachers can be remedied if more focus is placed on building more positive relationships with them (Cassetta & Sawyer, 2015). There are many reasons why these negative relationships exist; however, one culprit is due to the presence of teacher bias that is heavily influenced by the negative racial stereotypes many teachers are exposed to about diverse racial groups in the world (Will, 2020). These biases then lead teachers to form assumptions about the inclusion of diverse voices and perspectives and the value of diverse groups causing teachers to view students and their families' cultural differences through a cultural deficit lens (Valencia, 2010). Finally, teachers who explicitly or implicitly act on these biases and assumptions often project their lowered expectations onto students, leading to stereotypes that diminish the academic performance of the students who experience it (Steele, 1995). Teachers, we have to do better. However, we can't do better unless we know better. Many teachers aren't even aware of the negative attitudes they hold about students and families who are different from themselves. Thankfully, educational scholars offer a promising practice for helping teachers "see" what they "can't see" through regular and intentional self-reflective processes (Gay & Kirkland, 2003).

Giving teachers ongoing opportunities for reflective thinking about their relationship-building efforts should be commonplace in teacher professional development (Gay & Kirkland, 2003; Grice, 2019/2020). When done with purpose, intention, and humility, this type of self-reflection has the power to transform teachers into culturally caring educators who are aware of and responsive to the needs of all of their students (Grice, 2019/2020). Teachers should regularly examine how their own beliefs influence their beliefs about how they perceive the image and culture of a "good" student. They need to know how their assumptions and knowledge influence how they teach, what they teach, who and where they teach, and how they interact with diverse students and families. It must be clear during these reflections: Teachers cannot build relationships with and have collaborative interactions among those they fear, hate, pity, or view in deficit or inferior ways. If we find that we have negative perceptions of those different than ourselves, we must be willing to challenge the negative assumptions we hold and be prepared to replace them with more positive, accurate, and complete understandings by getting to know our students for who they really are.

Part of this begins with changing the narrative on how we describe student achievement or underachievement. Too often, teachers and schools describe the issues in public education as a problem that rests only within those who are experiencing the problem. For example, standardized test scores have become the barometer for achievement in public education. Although these tests have been proven to not be good indicators of student intellect or achievement (Mulholland, 2015), they have also been identified as racially biased and to favor middle-class, White norms (Whan Choi, 2020). Although this research is readily available and has been circulated among many education circles for decades, when those test scores come in and we see the disparities in racial and class groups, we don't say these tests need to be fixed (or done away with), we say these students need to be "fixed." We then frame this issue as a supposed "achievement gap" and insinuate that the students experiencing it are the ones lacking. The term "gap" implies that these students have failed to meet the requirements. But have they? If the tests they take are not relevant to their culture and class backgrounds, and exclude their knowledge, frames of reference, and performance styles (Gay, 2010), how else do we expect them to perform?

Many equity scholars and educators counter this narrative of the racial achievement gap and reframe it for what it is: an opportunity gap (Gorski, 2016). The same can be said when looking at building relationships with students experiencing academic or behavioral challenges. Is it that these students are just unmotivated, unreachable, or unmanageable? No. There are no "bad" students, only those we have yet to build authentic, caring relationships, and connections with. So, who are those students we have yet to provide these opportunities to? A quick assessment of our knowledge of who our students are can give us an indication.

Take a moment to think about your *favorite* student. You know, the one who's struggling academically or struggling behaviorally. Can you list 5-7 things that you know about that student? Do they love baking or cooking with grandma on the weekends? Are they a video gamer? A songwriter? Do they perform in dance recitals on the weekends? If the extent of your knowledge of your students stops at what time they enter the classroom, if they're late, or the last letter grade they received on last week's test, then you don't know your students very well. Let's change that. Check out the list below of questions adapted from the *National Equity Project* that you can ask students or their parents to help you get a better understanding of who your students are to foster more positive relationships with them.

Questions for Developing Deeper Connection and Understanding with Students

1. What special activities and/or traditions do you do with your family?
2. Can you tell me about a special family meal you like to eat and why?
3. Who are you close to in your family? Who do you wish you were closer to?
4. What radio stations do you listen to? Who is your favorite music artist?
5. Do you play sports, video games, or any other activities in or outside of school?
6. What do you like to read? If reading is not your favorite activity, can you tell me why?
7. What makes you happy? Sad? Angry?
8. What makes you feel safe?
9. What makes you embarrassed? How do you react when upset?
10. Who do you look up to? Why?
11. What is something you are proud of?

The point is, greater efforts can and should be made to interrupt the assumptions about our students and more emphasis placed on valuing who they really are.

Creating and maintaining positive, caring, and authentic relationships with students should be a top priority for every teacher. Building these successful and authentic relationships with our students that reflect trust, positive rapport, affirmation of their value, and validation of their needs and interests are non-negotiables in our attempts to embrace all students (Hammond, 2015). However, our students shouldn't just be able to see our efforts to build positive relationships with them through kind words and smiles. We must also be willing to listen to them when they say they are being treated unfairly or cruelly (Woodard, 2019). The natural result of a positive relationship between any two people will ultimately mean not just treating each other with dignity and respect, but standing up for them in the face of injustice and oppression at the hands of others, even if the "other" is us.

Engaging in the Elimination of Racist, Discriminatory, or Oppressive Policies

For more than a century, the U.S. public school system has struggled to create and maintain positive and equitable school experiences for all students (Anderson, 1988; Tyack, 1974; Woodson, 1933). Although early scholars in education such as John Dewey emphasized public education as a way to obtain more democratic educational experiences (Dewey, 1897), scholars such as Carter G. Woodson (1933) reminded us that more often than not, U.S. public school institutions have been places of racism, segregation, discrimination, and exclusion of nondominant peoples and ideas. Schools have had less of an emancipatory effect on marginalized students and more reminiscent of indoctrination and control (Slattery, 2013). Unfortunately, these issues weren't left in the past in the pages of history, as racism and discrimination are not only alive and well in society today, it runs freely about within our classrooms and schools, too.

Discussing these issues of racism in schools and society is difficult for many people to engage in. Many of us have been socialized to think that pointing out or mentioning race or instances of racism is the *real* crime. In reality, this works to silence those who speak out about its presence which leaves racist practices intact and unchallenged. Many teachers fall into the category of those who wish not to discuss or "see" racism, and as a result, students who are often the direct target of racism in today's schools are left to fend for themselves.

Recently, one student in a nearby Texas school was also left to fend for himself when his school decided that the locs he had been growing for years were not appropriate for a graduation ceremony and told him to cut his hair or forfeit the thirteen years of work he'd accomplished in school and miss his graduation (Cox, 2020). The boy and his parents refused to comply, and the school maintained they were simply following the rules which had been established years before. Unwilling to admit any wrongdoing or racial insensitivity by enforcing this rule, the young boy faced suspension instead. Many teachers who commented on this story sided with the school. To them, this was just a matter of non-compliance, not racism, as many stated they just couldn't "see it." Many racist and discriminatory school policies go unchallenged for this very reason. Too many teachers, administrators, and school leaders are ill-equipped to identify racism (and issues of inequity) because they don't even know what racism or inequity is or looks like.

Let us begin with a formal definition of racism. It is described by anti-racist educators and scholars Louise Derman-Sparks and Carol Brunson Phillips (1997) as "an institutionalized system of economic, political, social, and cultural relations that ensures one racial group has and maintains power and privilege over all others in all aspects of life" (p. 2). These aspects include but are not limited to healthcare, housing, employment, business, education, and wealth, among others. The manifestations of racism can not only come in the form of institutionalized and structural practices such as segregation or redlining, but it can also be enforced interpersonally and internally (Salter et al., 2018). Yes, individuals both consciously and unconsciously can participate in and reinforce racism. This is done when the individual reinforces the aforementioned relations in their interactions with nondominant peoples or upon their own marginalized status (Greer & Spalding, 2017). The term "reverse racism" has also crept into conversations about racism and tried to divert accountability of those accused of racism with less success.

Reverse racism is a belief often held by certain White individuals that the current strides towards racial equity has come at their expense (Norton & Sommers, 2011). It is the belief that any progress (as little as it may be) towards overturning racial inequality will now result in discrimination or anti-White bias, which negatively impacts White people. The Norton and Sommers (2011) study on this phenomenon revealed that this belief in reverse racism is so strong in many White Americans that they believed reverse racism to be a greater problem than the 500- year history of anti-black, anti-immigrant, and anti-indigenous racism in America.

To this point, it is true that nondominant people can also reinforce or be complicit in racism among their own people and against themselves as they have been socialized in a racist society as descendants of colonized groups. Slave drivers were often other enslaved people, and there are plenty of people of color in politics who often impose policies that oppress their own people (Kendi, 2019). Ibram X. Kendi's (2019) book *How to be an Antiracist* makes an interesting argument in challenging the "powerless defense" that many people of color ascribe to, which cites they can't be "racist" because they have no institutional power. Advocates of reverse racism would disagree. Although this point can and has been taken out of context to loosen the institutionalized grip that White racism (and white supremacy) plays in the lives of nondominant groups, it ultimately highlights the inherent complexities of racism and the many players in its insidious game. Fortunately, the pages of history tell a different story as no progress aimed at creating greater racial equity outcomes has yet to come close to dismantling the hold that White supremacy and power have on America (Jones, 2021).

Nonetheless, wherever you stand in the debate of who can and can't be racist, the point is that racism does exist, and it has negative and long-term effects on those exposed to it, even those who benefit from it.

It also can come in many forms and be expressed in many different ways. Unfortunately, many are not privy to these diverse manifestations and remain under the guise that racism is easy to spot and a racist even easier.

Many teachers, particularly White teachers, hold firmly to the belief that if something is presented kindly or is endorsed by People of Color, it cannot be deemed racist. For many of these educators, their understanding of racism and, therefore, who can be a racist, has left them with the impressions that these instances and perpetrators are only mean, vile, or explicitly violent people (DiAngelo, 2018). At the same time, "meanness" is less often attributed to the one practicing more subtle forms of racism, and is solely reserved for the one calling it out, especially the Person of Color (Metta, 2016). As an educator who practiced anti-racism in her classroom long before it was trendy to do so, I am well aware of how often the "angry Black woman" trope is used in an attempt to silence the Black racism whistleblower. Many educators find it hard to identify racism and racist practices because they cling too tightly to the stereotype that "nice" equals non-racist, instead of challenging themselves to become aware of all forms of racism and removing the threat by therefore becoming anti-racist (Kendi, 2019).

In the following quote, Austin Channing Brown (2018) illustrates how ugly valuing "niceness" over anti-racism can be:

> In my experience, white people who believe they are safe often prove dangerous when that identity is challenged. This is partly because most white people still believe that they are good and true racists are easy to spot...When you believe niceness disproves the presence of racism, it's easy to start believing bigotry is rare, and that the label should only be applied to mean-spirited, intentional acts of discrimination. The problem with this framework--besides being a gross misunderstanding of how racism operates in systems and structures enabled by nice people---is that it obligates me to be nice in return, rather than truthful. I am expected to come closer to the racists. Be nicer to them. Coddle them (p. 101).

The coddling stops here. Many efforts in schools to identify and eliminate racist practices and policies have been silenced as feelings and the discomfort (particularly White folks) about discussions of racism have taken priority (DiAngelo, 2018). The mental and emotional acrobatics that ensue when attempting to discuss issues of racism with some White people have discouraged many anti-racist advocates from even attempting to do so (Eddo-Lodge, 2014). I, too, have felt the overwhelming sense of frustration when trying to explain the experiences of a Black woman in America, only to have those experiences gaslighted or deemed imaginary. I, too, have been tempted to stop talking to some White people and People of Color who refuse to try to understand about racism. But for the sake of my students and my very own children, I can't stop talking about racism in America, especially regarding education. Racism is real, and to end it, we have to be more committed to its unveiling than its cover-up.

Whether we are comfortable or not, educators who are committed to creating positive environments for all students have to engage in the work of understanding how race and oppression work in society and schools. This work is hard, and this work is challenging, but this work is the backbone in educators being effective in identifying harmful and discriminatory policies and practices in their schools. Again, the scope of this book is not designed to address all of the racial identity legwork needed to be done in order for educators to understand their position in a racist society such as the U.S. and the steps needed to take to move towards anti-racism. However, books like Beverly Daniel Tatum's (1997) *Why Are All the Black Kids Sitting Together in the Cafeteria?* and Ijeoma Oluo's (2018) *So You Want to Talk About Race* can help with those first steps. Brittney Cooper's (2019) *Eloquent Rage* is a helpful guide in self-reflection towards anti-racist action as a follow-up. Even so, this book is committed to making sure educators are focused on equity, the process of challenging inequitable policies, and replacing them with more equitable solutions.

For teachers dedicated to creating fair and equitable school policies, we must be able to assess our school climates in matters of equity and inclusion. These assessments can come in the form of formal or informal methods. Surveys sent home to teachers, students, their families, and the community about the school climate can be very effective in understanding what needs to be addressed first. Asking students if they feel safe at school or asking caregivers if they view the staff as welcoming and authentically caring can be huge wake-up calls for schools who thought "niceness" was good enough. Often, students and their families have a better view of inequities in schools because they are the direct targets of racist and/or discriminatory policies and practices. Evaluating the disparities in the demographic responses can be telling as well. If one demographic of students and families cites more negative experiences at school than others, this is a good opportunity to reconcile those disparities with a more culturally responsive approach. If something more formal is needed, hiring an equity consultant offers schools a more in-depth look at their school practices to determine which policies are outdated, and need to be reevaluated to produce more equitable outcomes. However, equitable policies are only as good as the equity capacity of those that enforce them.

Secondly, we must also be able to assess ourselves. Educators and school leaders can work together to ensure that teachers are engaging in ongoing practices that heighten their understanding of all forms of explicit and implicit bias, historically and currently. They must be willing to challenge themselves and other school community members in addressing these issues as well. Teachers must break the social stigma chains that calling attention to racism is worse than the actual racism. We must get over our fears of being identified as a "racist" and understand that many happen. We live in a racist society and have been conditioned to think, act, and believe racist ideas. Hopefully, in this awakening, we can also work together to create more positive and antiracist environments instead of withering under the weight of perceived attacks on our moral character and goodness. We have to be willing to make mistakes, but know that these mistakes are part of the process and proof that we are on our way to better days ahead. School leaders can help with this fear by creating school communities focused on creating collective accountability. If one member or a group is struggling, it should be the job of others more skilled or further along in their racial understanding to help the other, not tear them apart. We must know that equity is hard, and anti-racism work is even harder. If it was easy, it would already be in place. It will take prolonged effort and commitment on behalf of schools and their communities to make sure it remains a priority and a foundation in all they do.

Creating environments that embrace all students is key in creating equitable environments for every student. Building school climates that are dedicated to creating welcoming and affirming atmospheres, building positive and authentic relationships, and identifying, addressing, and removing racist and discriminatory practices within schools is a non-negotiable. To do this, we have to be willing to put the needs of our students first. Just as a doctor cannot be an effective surgeon if they cannot advocate for the needs of their patients, schools in today's multiracial society cannot be effective in educating diverse students if they do not commit to eradicating all forms of individual and structural oppression, inequality, and discrimination present within classrooms and schools. Schools committed to these practices will be better equipped to meet all needs of students and create greater pathways for achievement. Ultimately, a school's ability to work together with teachers, students, and families will be the glue that holds these efforts together. A strong concept of community and collaboration will be key in creating equitable environments through empowering students.

Questions for Reflection

1. Assess the school climate at your campus? Is it positive? Do all students and families feel welcome and included?
2. Think about a student you have had difficulty with in the past. How was your relationship with that student? Do you think you really knew that student authentically, or were there important elements of their culture or identity you wish you had more knowledge of?
3. What policies or practices in your school should be reevaluated for equity? After this recognition, who do you need to include in this evaluation in order to make the necessary changes?

3. EMPOWERING ALL STUDENTS

"One cannot expect positive results from an educational or political action program which fails to respect the particular view of the world held by the people. Such a program constitutes cultural invasion, good intentions notwithstanding."

— PAULO FREIRE, *PEDAGOGY OF THE OPPRESSED*

The most amazing example of an empowering school culture is the story of Geoffrey Canada's *Harlem Children's Zone Project*. Since the 1990s, Canada's ambitious project to provide high-quality learning and support for all students in the Harlem area is an example of the powerful possibilities in store for many schools wanting to make a difference in the lives of their students. His project provides comprehensive education and community services for children and families from birth to college and has successfully served the needs of over 14,000 students and their families. Canada's success in helping his historically marginalized community of poor and low-income Black American families is a success story we should all support. To his credit, one of the most telling components of this program's success for over 20 years has been his dedication to building up and working with students *and* their families to support them in the areas they need most (Yeung, 2008).

Canada's successful project highlights the important understanding that an empowering school culture is a collaborative one! Building collaborative relationships with students, families, and their communities is a critical element in helping students and families make the positive changes they hope to see in education and the world! This kind of education does not just teach "the standards" but allows students to think critically and question their learning environments. It also empowers them to remove any barriers that prevent students from receiving fair and equitable learning opportunities. Ultimately, an empowering school is the embodiment of positive change by advocating for their students and their families and working together with them to manifest the changes they wish to see in the world. Schools successful in this endeavor have let go of the traditional relationship model between families and schools of deference to what schools want, and control of parent involvement initiatives, and have traded them in for ones rooted in building equitable collaborations and utilizing the cultural capital which rests within each student and family they serve.

Developing Collaborative Partnerships with Parents, Families, and the Community

I recently released some research about the importance of building collaborative partnerships with families in an article published in the *Journal for Multicultural Affairs* entitled "Perceptions of Family Engagement between African American Families and Schools: A Review of Literature" (Grice, 2020). Although my research was specific to African American students and their families, what follows are important considerations when attempting to build relationships between schools, students, and their families that can be utilized for other nondominant groups as well. This research is important as it highlights the social stigma many African American families experience when their family engagement style does not match what is expected by the school. This cultural mismatch then places families in a position to have their child(ren) and themselves experience lower expectations and negative treatment by educators as a result. Closing the gap in understanding the culturally diverse ways families *do* participate is key in creating collaborative family-school partnerships.

In this research, I point out that the continued presence of racial disparities in achievement (NCES, 2017b), discipline rates (Kunjufu, 2012), and special education referrals among marginalized students (Delpit, 2006) intensifies the need to strengthen the relationships between diverse families and schools. Although there are many complex issues that can contribute to these outcomes, such as poverty (Books, 2007), lack of qualified teachers, lack of resources, and lower-quality curriculum (Darling-Hammond, 2010), increased parental involvement and improved family-school relationships for marginalized students is a promising solution to help mitigate the destructiveness of these realities (Latunde, 2018).

Throughout the research, I highlight the effects of increased family engagement on student achievement and indicators that parental involvement increases academic achievement and positive outcomes in personal and social areas (Brandon, 2007; Yamauchi et al., 2017). These outcomes can include higher grades and graduation rates, increased satisfaction with school and attendance, fewer retentions, and the reduction of disciplinary actions such as suspensions and detentions (Henderson & Mapp, 2002; Sheldon & Epstein, 2002). Decades of research on the topics of parental involvement and parent engagement have been instrumental in helping schools remove barriers to this important component of academic success and create greater pathways towards collaboration between families and schools (Baker et al., 2016; Epstein, 2011; Miller et al., 2013; Norris, 2018).

However, it has been problematic to utilize these terms interchangeably as "parent involvement" has been described as the actions parents take to participate in school-sponsored, school-based activities and events (Jeynes, 2013); while "parental engagement" notates a partnership between schools and families where parental concerns are heard, addressed, and used to create positive learning environments for their students (Ferlazzo, 2011). The term "parent involvement" also often limits the participants of these traditional school-based activities to the child's parent and fails to consider the many home-based interventions many diverse parents seek to participate in and the extended family that is often involved as well (Yamauchi et al., 2017). Also problematic are the traditional concepts of "parent involvement" and "parent engagement," which have often been used to describe the needs of the school and the ways in which they want parents to participate and support their students (Baker et al., 2016; Norris, 2018). This practice is exclusionary, one-sided, hierarchical, and ignores the diverse needs of the families schools serve (Goldsmith & Robinson Kurpius, 2018; Lasater, 2019).

Family-School Partnerships

However, the use of the term "family-school partnerships" focuses on the understanding that parental involvement/engagement with the school should be a collaborative effort and that the perspectives of the parent and the school should be included in the decision-making process. Family-school partnerships are defined as relationships that are:

[D]esigned and executed with an intentional focus on the home-school interface and constructive connections between families and educators...partnership actions include collaboration, cooperation, consistent messaging, planned and coordinated strategies across home and school, and home-school information-sharing and communication (Smith et al., 2020, p. 513).

This term also opens up the notion of who can be considered part of a family and school collaboration by including the often-unnoted participants in a child's education, such as siblings and other extended family members (Yamauchi et al., 2017). Essentially, authentic family-school partnerships reflect "respectful alliances among educators, families, and community groups that value relationship building, dialogue, and power-sharing as part of socially just, democratic schools" (Auerbach, 2010, p. 729). Utilizing the goals of developing family-school partnerships as a focus, increasing parental engagement among diverse student populations becomes attainable and is responsive to the needs of not only the school, but the families and students as well.

Unfortunately, my research underscores the numerous barriers in this endeavor (Cooper, 2009; Peck & Reitzug, 2018). Many of the forms of parental engagement schools encourage are typically based on White, middle-class, and school-based activities such as attending conferences, participating in booster clubs, and other on-site contributions (Boonk et al., 2018). To remedy this, schools committed to serving diverse students and families must adopt more inclusive and culturally aware understandings of the multiple ways in which diverse families support their child's education (Baker et al., 2016).

To begin, schools must challenge the common misconception that parents of marginalized students do not value education if they do not replicate White, middle-class practices. Teachers must also let go of their false assumptions when discussing the issues contributing to the struggles of their low-income, African American, Latinx, or Native American students when they cite a lack of care or commitment from parents (Cooper, 2009). It's just not true. There are many studies, along with the combined history of nondominant groups' fight for access to high-quality and equitable education, which indicate that these families not only care about education but often take great risks to obtain the rights to the education they and their children deserve (Cokely, 2014; Hale-Benson & Hilliard, 1986). Unfortunately, many teachers' understandings of nondominant families have been tainted by deficit views rendering many unable to view these families from a strength-based lens (Cooper, 2009; Wilson & Yull, 2018). The process of closing the gaps in these perceptions and allowing teachers to see the value in the culturally relevant ways that nondominant families participate will be key in mending these long-tattered relationships. It is essential for teachers to grow in their knowledge of the cultural capital students and families possess, and to utilize this information to create collaborative and equitable school partnerships based on meeting the needs of every party involved (Ishiumaru, 2020). In an empowering school, gone are the days of schools dictating to students and families what's best for them and strict adherence to dominant norms and structures. For true educational empowerment, collaboration, and change to happen, schools must "initiate educational change with nondominant families and communities---and center their priorities, concerns, expertise, knowledge, and resources (rather than that of the system, or of white, middle-class parents or educators)"; only then "can we begin to counter the status quo normative assumptions in the system about what and who matters" (Ishimaru, 2020, p. 51).

To accomplish this, teachers can begin to grow their knowledge of the cultures, perspectives, and experiences of nondominant peoples by participating in local community events to help develop a positive foundation for future relationships. These future relationships with community members can help to identify needs and services for families such as parenting classes, financial literacy, or English language services (New York State Education Department, 2019). For students, these community events can be used as field trips to help foster students' connections to their surrounding community. Places like museums or cultural centers are great places to foster and instill a love for community among students (New York State Education Department, 2019).

For creating greater pathways to share power and include the expertise of families in school decisions, create parent-led advisory groups which work together with teachers, students, families, and community members to establish school values and expectations within the school (New York State Education Department, 2019). Another important finding that came out of my research on family-school partnerships helps put this point into perspective. A study on the effects of one type of parent advisory initiative by Wilson and Yull (2018) found that a Parent Mentor Program in which African American parents were assigned as mentors to help in the classrooms of the schools their students attend provided promising active engagement strategies any school can emulate. Their study not only had a positive impact on the students, but resulted in creating more positive interactions and experiences between the teachers and the parents as well. Their approach in utilizing African American parents as mentors in the classroom changed the perceptions of the teachers in seeing them as "problems," and now saw them as important assets in helping them understand the needs of their students.

Having these multiple perspectives when gauging the needs of students will enable the implementation of policies and practices that are culturally relevant and responsive to many families while still aiming for school-wide goals and initiatives of equity and student success. Forming these diverse and collaborative groups between families and schools will be more effective in meeting the needs of every student and family in the building. Equally important to the success of these initiatives will be the methods of communication established between families and schools (Smith, 2020). Incorporating more diverse ways of communication can include providing materials in multiple languages, through multiple means, and across multiple platforms. Schools should consider more flexible ways to reach out to parents (and have parents reach in) by making communication compatible with family's language, digital or in-person preferences, by phone, text, email, or allowing walk-in conference times (Bordalba & Bochaca, 2019). Not only that, but focusing on increasing more positive communication opportunities is helpful. Many families of marginalized backgrounds often complain about the negative manner in which school personnel speak to them when addressing concerns regarding their children. It is important to remember that barriers to positive communication do not only come in the form of *what* we use to communicate with but also *how* we choose to communicate with our students and families as well (Gibson & Haight, 2013; Powell & Coles, 2021).

Ultimately, an empowering school culture allows all parties involved to have a say in the daily happenings of the environment. Schools committed to an empowering school atmosphere will welcome the voices of teachers, students, families, and the community to ensure that every stakeholder feels included and that their needs and concerns are considered in school practices and policies. Only by schools and families working together can positive gains in efforts to build relationships between families and schools happen.

Developing a Sense of Agency in Students

I often like to quote the words of Indian lawyer and social activist Mahatma Gandhi when he said, "Be the change you want to see in the world." Unfortunately, after diving into some more research into this cultural icon of non-violence and anti-colonialism, I discovered this famed quote to be untrue (Ranseth, 2017). It's not untrue in the sense that the sentiment rings false. It's untrue in the sense that Gandhi never actually muttered those particular words; instead he said something much more profound:

> We but mirror the world. All the tendencies present in the outer world are to be found in the world of our body. If we could change ourselves, the tendencies in the world would also change. As a man changes his own nature, so does the attitude of the world change toward him. This is the divine mystery supreme. A wonderful thing it is and the source of our happiness. We need not wait to see what others do.
>
> — MAHATMA GANDHI

These words, though more reflective and thought-provoking, still point us in the same direction. If we want to see positive changes in our world, we have to first change ourselves. Creating change in any capacity can be difficult. Creating change among human beings who are prone to a nature that resists change is even harder, but not impossible (Fowler, 2017). Nonetheless, this sentiment is still very helpful in understanding how to create empowering school cultures and positive change in our educational institutions. It is also important in helping us to guide our students in creating positive changes in their classrooms and in the world. To do this, we've got to be able to come to terms with the issues many students face in this world and be prepared to engage in the difficult dialogues about the inequalities they see and the actions needed to help us begin to create the change in attitude and action that can really make *their* world a better place.

Unfortunately, many teachers have reservations about discussing political issues and politics that plague students' everyday lives. Even more teachers are ill-equipped to do so, as the average teacher hails from demographic backgrounds and vastly different experiences than the average student (Will, 2020a). With 79 percent of the teaching population still overwhelmingly White, middle-class, and female and over half the student population representing nondominant groups, these disparities play a larger role in meeting the needs of students than we like to admit (Will, 2020b). However, as the political waters around us grow murkier and murkier, all teachers who claim a sense of social responsibility to develop students into active global citizens are looking for ways to engage in critical dialogues with students without sinking into these torrential muddy waters. Although some teachers have chosen to engage with their students without filters by using derogatory language (Daniels, 2019), doing so could have devastating consequences on an educator's career and students' development.

On the other hand, some teachers and districts are so tight-lipped about issues in the world for fear of being seen as "too political," that critical conversations about issues in the world are nearly non-existent in their teaching. Today, let's put some balance between these two extremes. Teachers, if we want students to grow up to be engaged citizens able to think critically about the world around them, shouldn't we be able to effectively do it ourselves first?

The resistance in upsetting the status quo in any manner can be formidable and fierce. My personal stances on creating anti-racist and anti-bias classroom environments for my students have often upset stakeholders who hold traditional "American" values and beliefs. I consider the backlash is worth it in order to create more positive experiences for students and families whose voices often go unnoticed and unheard in school settings. Being a teacher that is an agent of change and has a greater sense of social responsibility, one does not look at teaching as an objective, decontextualized act of simply transferring knowledge to students. The critical approach necessary in teaching towards social responsibility allows teachers and students to be more than regurgitators of facts, but critical thinkers of their world, able to critique current systems and work towards justice, peace, equity, and equality for all.

Introducing or discussing what can be seen as controversial issues in the classroom should not be done lightly. There can be implications and consequences for teachers who challenge the status quo in many school environments. As misinformed legislative attempts to silence or ban teachers from taking this approach are becoming more frequent (Camera, 2021); it should be understood that this process is not about making students think the way we want them to think; in fact, it is the freedom of guiding them in *how* to think more critically about the issues they face (Ladson-Billings, 1995). As agents of change in today's classroom, we are to help guide students in using difficult dialogues to promote peace and justice. Tackling controversial issues in the classroom can be daunting. In this "age of outrage" and "virtue signaling," the waters have been muddied even more in understanding what issues are morally imperative and must be considered in teaching with a critical approach (Brown & Lee, 2015).

Consider the following suggestions on how to set up a classroom environment where tackling sensitive issues can be done thoughtfully and respectfully. First, keep an open mind. We should be able to set a tone that says students should and will be able to learn about issues and positions from multiple points of view. We must also be able to value the different cultural norms each student brings into the class. Not everyone will value the same ways of thinking, acting, or behaving in the classroom, so we must maintain respect for the diversity of cultural patterns. This practice allows space for the challenging of dominant views, which often overshadow the perspectives and experiences of nondominant groups who are often harmed by policies and practices in different ways.

Next, model and show respect. Teachers should aim to create an atmosphere that shows respect for differing opinions and beliefs. It's not always about who's right and who's wrong. Instead, focus on students getting practice in disagreeing with others respectfully and understanding that doing so does not always mean letting go of personal convictions. This means acknowledging the multiple perspectives and experiences of fellow students. This also means understanding that certain topics are going to seem offensive to certain students. In this dilemma, consider *how* you offend and approach issues that could be polarizing with as balanced a perspective as possible. Although all sides should be recognized and heard, the goal should not be to keep people comfortable in their bigotry but to challenge it and address it. No students' value, personhood, right to exist, etc., should be diminished or threatened in these discussions. Period.

Lastly, work hard to establish a sense of morality and shared ethics in the classroom. However, I caution that this can be tricky. Because we want classrooms that maintain a sense of respect for all people and beliefs, we also need to maintain a positive classroom environment. If students express ideas, opinions, or beliefs that articulate the dehumanization, erasure, or marginalization of another group, we must be ready to challenge those stances. If we aim to teach greater equity, love, and acceptance in the world, we must be able to stand against hate, bigotry, and oppression in the process, even if it comes from our colleagues, students, or their families. It can be difficult to express dissent regarding traditional "American" beliefs, which are often rooted in discrimination and marginalization of nondominant groups. The emphasis on individualism and meritocracy has made it more difficult to come together as a community and remove barriers that restrict access to opportunities for others. We have been hard-wired to believe that smart, hardworking people have success, and if you are struggling, then you must not be smart or hardworking. If we are not aware of the marginalization that many so-called "traditional" beliefs result in for our diverse students and their families, we are not simply being neutral; we are being *complicit* in continuing their oppression. Therefore, we must be knowledgeable of the unequal distribution of power in our society and our classroom (Villegas & Lucas, 2002). Our students hail from many different economic, social, and religious backgrounds, and we must help students feel empowered in bridging the gaps that separate countries, political structures, religions, and values by valuing not only a dominant perspective but marginalized ones as well. Ultimately, we have to consider how we promote and model the act of critical thinking of complex issues. Remember, sometimes there are no neutral positions; sometimes wrong is wrong no matter how "traditional" or "American" the idea may seem. Additionally, whether we agree with this understanding or not, we have to come to an understanding that all teaching is a political act. Anytime we take a stance to speak up or remain silent, we are sending a message. The question remains: what messages are you choosing to send to your diverse students about the issues that affect them most?

If we are truly agents of change working to make the world a better place, we must be able to reflect on the areas in our teaching practices that do not measure up to those goals. Let's take action! Think about a topic that you usually shy away from in your classroom: racism, sexism, homophobia, immigration, white supremacy, white privilege, police brutality, climate change, etc. How can you grow in your understanding of these issues and present them to your students from a multiple perspectives approach? How can your simple act of engaging in difficult dialogues embody a vision of a better world for your students? Not only that, but after the dialogues are over, how will you move your students to action? There's no point in talking about issues and inequities if we are not serious about taking action to eradicate them. So, what's your action plan?

In taking action, we must be able to consider the learning opportunities we present to our students that will allow them to move toward a desired sense of agency and take action against the many societal ills they face. For educators, it means that the learning experiences we provide must be rooted in understanding topics of power, privilege, access, and opportunity. This foundational knowledge base is crucial in cultivating our students' ability to recognize and redress inequities within the classroom, within the school, and within their communities (Gorski, 2019). These learning opportunities can come in the form of project-based activities that focus on relevant and meaningful circumstances that students are facing in the present and actively identifying and dismantling all forms of inequity they see (New York State Education Department, 2019).

Many teachers are already taking on this task as they create math lessons that use statistics and algebra to assess economic inequity; science lessons that investigate the effects of capitalism on climate change; reading and writing assignments that bring in marginalized voices and perspectives; and even art and music lessons centered around the critique of works which center social justice movements. National Teacher of the Year Jahana Hayes knows the power of these learning opportunities as she promotes community service and cultural awareness activities throughout her history lessons (Borrello, 2016). Her students have participated in projects with Habitat for Humanity, autism walks, and food pantry donations. She says these projects help her students realize how capable they are of not only making change, but accomplishing great things! Any of these ideas and more can help our students make critical connections about the world to their learning by providing them opportunities to participate in learning experiences that reflect the issues they care about most! Let's get planning!

I find it ironic that as I sit and type these words, the U.S. is experiencing another attack on its democracy in the form of white rage. As some Americans sat in shock at seeing White rioters scale walls, break windows, and utterly attempt to destroy the U.S. Capitol building, others more familiar with the reactions of White mobs when they feel their power is being challenged were less moved. To help students make sense of the events unfolding, critical educators are sharing ideas and discussing ways to connect this most recent example of White rage with past eruptions during the Civil War, Reconstruction, Red Summer, and the Civil Rights Movement (Bradley, 2021).

In the aftermath of COVID-19, the recognition of structural forms of privilege, power, historical, and contemporary inequities have become front and center. Job loss has affected over 20 million Americans all at once (Kochhar, 2020), and many Americans who once held deeply to the idea that welfare recipients and food stamp awardees were "lazy" or culturally deficient are experiencing what it's like to be hungry, jobless, and struggling with mental health, among other issues (Friedman, 2020). As a result, schools have worked to provide meals, access to necessary technology, acted as temporary testing sites, and provided for needs in their communities, all while dealing with COVID-19 outbreaks among teachers and students! Needless to say, it is very clear that power and privilege have always played a role in who has access to what they need and who doesn't (Aschoff, 2020; Solomon, 2020). Many of our students are even more aware of it, too.

As online learning has taken center stage across many schools in America, what better way than to integrate those necessary learning objectives into the everyday curriculum to help students understand how to create positive change in the world they see. Projects that include analyzing the access to supplies like toilet paper, bottled water, and other groceries would be a great substitute for a boring review on a math worksheet. To keep students' writing skills intact, implement journaling to share their diverse experiences and release the many mixed and uneasy emotions they feel during this unprecedented time. Science lessons could include alternative meal prep experiments. As many do not have everything they need to create complete meals, asking students to get creative with ingredients allows them to shine if they are already cooking geniuses and creates an opportunity for others to learn a new skill. Aligning the everyday experiences of students with their curriculum is not hard to do if we know who our students are, what they are experiencing, and what they want to do to make positive changes around them. Learning about plant life cycles? Grow a garden and donate the food to local food pantries. Teaching about financial literacy? Start a small business with your students that helps meet the needs of the students on campus. Doing a unit on data collection? Have your students administer a survey on bullying. Find out who is being bullied, why, and discuss ways to reduce its occurrence. Finding out which students feel most marginalized or isolated can make way for coalition or student advocacy groups to support those who are struggling. The opportunities are endless!

Moving students towards active engagement in change-making

endeavors doesn't have to be viewed as extra, optional, or inappropriate for the learning environment. It should be deemed essential! If our classrooms are not places where students can learn and grow in their understanding of diverse perspectives and experiences, can we even say we've produced 21st-century learners? There is no learning if circumstances don't change, and there is no true education if the instruction received does not ignite a fire to grow and do better. Any true education has not only the power to grow us and change us, but also to uplift us to empower ourselves and others.

Creating an Empowering School Culture

The theme of empowerment cannot be stressed enough throughout this chapter. Its essential elements of collective collaboration, mutual accountability, and student and family advocacy should be essential for establishing equitable relationships and positive school environments. Truly transformative schools committed to uplifting and empowering all students and families are always aiming to help "develop a sense of power and demonstrate an ability to influence the environments that affect people's lives" (Koren et al., 1992; Pearson et al., 2019). True empowerment is essential for creating and maintaining equity in schools through collaboration as it is needed to "reduce families' feelings of powerlessness and enable them to take appropriate action to resolve problems" (Pearson et al., 2019, p. 211). This is important because when parents and families feel a sense of empowerment, they become better advocates for their needs and the needs of their children (Pearson et al., 2019). For nondominant groups of students and their families, empowering school cultures are necessary to overturn many of the current practices and policies that favor mainstream and dominant group norms and needs at their expense. In creating these empowering climates, prioritizing the needs of traditionally marginalized students and families is key. In doing so, teachers and schools must effectively understand the diverse needs of their students and families by utilizing two important approaches: cultural responsiveness and cultural reciprocity.

Culturally responsive teaching, which seeks to use the "cultural knowledge, prior experiences, frames of reference, and performance styles of ethnically diverse students," can create empowering schools by transforming teachers into culturally competent mediators who can utilize knowledge, values, and beliefs of nondominant families to make classroom and school environments responsive their diverse needs (Gay, 2010, p. 31). Within these culturally responsive relationships, teachers will recognize the needs of diverse families, while empowering them to become greater participants in the school environment (Norris, 2018). One of the key components in helping teachers acquire a culturally responsive disposition is increasing their cultural competence, socio-political awareness, and self-reflective practices (Gooden & Dantley, 2012; Villegas & Lucas, 2002). Teachers' ability to understand the complex dynamics of the socio-political, cultural, historical, and economic forces that affect the lives of their students combined with intentional reflective thinking on their attitudes about diverse people will be non-negotiables in this practice. Perceptions of empowerment in nondominant families can be situated in a way that removes the common assumption of schools as the only "experts" and allows room for families to have their knowledge included in the structuring of the school as well (Wilson & Yull, 2018).

Cultural reciprocity works similarly but focuses more on educators not only understanding their students' and families' beliefs but their own beliefs as well. Cultural reciprocity asks teachers and families to identify their beliefs and discuss them, note similarities and differences, respect cultural differences, and collaborate with families to make recommendations that are more aligned with each family's values (Kalyanpur & Harry, 2012). Always cognizant of the varied and diverse needs of every student and family, these approaches work together to create the structural changes necessary to ensure all families have opportunity and access to greater educational success (Ishimaru, 2013). When all students and families have their needs and concerns taken into consideration, we create empowerment. When that empowerment turns into greater access to opportunity, we create true equity.

Recent research conducted by practitioners can provide us with a blueprint to ensure that the culturally responsive practices we introduce will allow us to create the empowering school culture we wish to obtain. Below is a list of strategies teachers and schools can use to make sure they are aiming for empowerment and keeping the overall goal of equity in mind as well.

Practices to Support an Empowering School Culture

- Keep classroom, school, and family practices and policies family-centered.
- Create opportunities to get to know families to address their values and concerns, respect cultural differences, and work together with them to adapt school practices and policies to be inclusive of their values and needs.
- Identify families' strengths and incorporate them into the services you provide.
- Respect the cultural values and each family's role in participating in advocacy efforts.
- Continually build on establishing relationships with students and families built on positive rapport and trust.
- Prioritize needs, interests, goals, and experiences of nondominant students and families.
- Match families' goals with information on resources in the school and community that can meet those needs.
- Practice multimodal communication allowing parents and families to communicate with you through means that it is accessible and convenient for them.
- Hire educators or partner with local organizations that can communicate in each family's native language. (Ishimaru, 2013; Khalifa, 2018; Pearson et al., 2019).

Creating empowering school cultures is foundational in making sure the needs of all students and families are met. No longer should the diverse needs of culturally and linguistically diverse (CLD) students and their families be ignored or remain in the margins of school improvement plans. No longer should schools simply wait for parents to get fed up with being ignored, which creates only reactionary results on the part of the school. Instead, schools should work to be proactive in approaches to working with diverse students and families and make it clear consistently throughout the school year that they are dedicated to meeting the needs of their families, and they have the structures, policies, and practices in place to do so.

Questions for Reflection

1. Reflect on your school environment. What are some variables of your school environment that need to be changed in order to create a more empowering school structure?
2. Which practices for supporting an empowering school structure does your campus already employ? Which practices can your campus work towards including in the future?
3. What problems might your campus or school encounter in trying to create a more empowering school climate?
4. What benefits might result for your students and families if your school can successfully create an empowering and collaborative school environment?

4. EDUCATING ALL STUDENTS

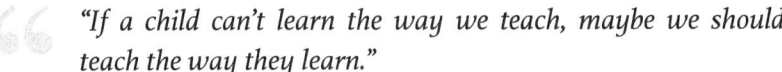
"If a child can't learn the way we teach, maybe we should teach the way they learn."

— IGNACIO ESTRADA

Quarantine life during COVID-19 has presented many challenges and opportunities for teachers and schools to rethink how they structure learning opportunities for their diverse student populations. With the immediate (and virtually overnight) thrust into online learning, many schools were frantically searching for ways to meet the needs of every student. In the midst of this thrust, questions about how to serve the very unique student populations on our campuses were now more important than ever. How will teachers support English language learners (ELLs)? How will students with individual education plans (IEPs) continue to receive their much-needed services? How will Special Education teachers meet the very real and often physical needs of the students in their care? Who will and who won't have access to internet services, laptop devices, or even the daily meals they relied on during school hours?

However, many of these issues are not new. Many of these questions have been in continuous circulation amongst many educators for years, even decades. Unfortunately, the immediacy was not always there. Students, parents, and community leaders have been advocating for far too long to have their voices heard and their students' educational needs and desires acknowledged and implemented. Quite often, funding issues, program inclusions, and supplemental aid and support for much-needed programs comes down to who needs it and who has the power to get it. To put this into perspective, a debate about the continuous need for Dual Language programs in the district where I once lived and worked came to a heated halt after a town hall meeting a few years ago. These programs, which were designed to help students learn through the strength of their first language (often Spanish) while also acquiring the necessary skill development of English, were an important part of scaffolding learning opportunities for the students enrolled in the program. Those in favor, such as parents, students, educators, and community members, pleaded with school officials during this meeting to keep the programs going (Benito, 2018). They cited the empirical evidence of the benefit of these programs as "Dual language programs foster bilingualism, biliteracy, enhanced awareness of linguistic and cultural diversity, and high levels of academic achievement through instruction in two languages" (Dual Language Education of New Mexico, 2020). All of which fell on deaf ears.

Their battle was lost as the school board members opposed the continuation of the program, as they couldn't fathom spending the little over $1 million the program cost to operate per year (Benito, 2018). Continuing to provide this much-needed, best-practice, culturally relevant, and academically beneficial learning opportunity for the majority Latinx/Hispanic students it served was too much for the district's budget. I guess I can understand the decision; if every school district went around spending money on the programs that helped every student achieve at high levels, there wouldn't be any money left over for football stadiums and pay raises for superintendents (read sarcasm). Sadly, this situation is not an anomaly. This is the painful reality for many underserved student groups.

Schools have always and will continue to decide whose learning needs will be met and whose won't. The historical and current underachievement trends for many marginalized students underscore the need for reform in the way schools make decisions on how they educate diverse students (NCES, 2017a). Advocating for school environments that foster high expectations, rigorous and culturally relevant curricula, and learning environments which utilize students' strengths are essential in making sure this happens. Instruction should also consider how different students learn and encourage students to take intellectual risks in growing in their understanding of the world around them. A 21st-century school does not just prepare students to succeed academically on standardized tests, but also to think critically and function positively cross-culturally in a growing global economy and world. To do this, the voices and needs of CLD students need to be included in the creation of school practices and policies that influence our curriculum. The low-quality curricula and low expectations that many marginalized students have experienced and continue to experience on behalf of teachers and schools should no longer remain pushed under the rug and covered up with surface-level approaches to diversity, but critically exposed and culturally responsive solutions put in place to reduce these negative occurrences in the future.

Utilizing Culturally Relevant Curricula and Resources

In my home state of Texas, curriculum reform efforts recently got a much-needed upgrade to its course offerings. Starting in the 2020-2021 school year, Texas high school students are allowed to choose (as an elective) an African American studies course to add to their existing required course schedule (Mendez, 2020). For many, this is a dream come true; for others, the first thing that comes to mind is 'What took ya'll so long?' To their point, this change comes two years after Texas's education agency moved to introduce a Mexican American Studies course which upset many at school board meetings as disagreements over not only the name of the course grew heated, but arguments over finding culturally relevant and historically accurate texts were present as well (C. Smith, 2019). The slow implementation of these kinds of learning opportunities in Texas schools, and schools across the nation, points to the long road ahead in implementing more as Native/Indigenous and Asian/Pacific Islander studies courses are still nonexistent. Only time will tell what disagreements will ensue with the implementation of this new African American studies update. Typically, these kinds of updates, even after they are passed, are sometimes poorly implemented. However contested, I wish that I could say that these disagreements over the addition of ethnic studies courses were new or unfounded. Sadly, that is not the case.

Unfortunately, integrating culturally relevant curricula into standard educational objectives has had a long fight in gaining acceptance in U.S. public schools. Over a century ago, scholars like W.E.B. DuBois called for the inclusion of Black history in schools; and during the Civil Rights Movement, Freedom Schools were erected to serve the purpose of instilling Black cultural roots in African American youth (Anderson, 2016). The fight for the inclusion of ethnic studies courses was also highly debated on college campuses across the country in San Francisco and other places (Meraji, 2019). More recently, state officials and school leaders were also in the fight against the inclusion of a Mexican American studies course in Tucson, Arizona, stating that such a curriculum is "toxic" and "divisive" (Anderson, 2016a). Truth be told, simply adding ethnic studies courses does nothing to create the much-needed widespread culturally responsive approaches that create greater access to equitable learning opportunities for all students. In spite of all of the benefits of doing so, such as decreases in dropout rates and increased academic achievement for traditionally marginalized students, many are still on the fence on the necessity of these courses (Anderson, 2016a).

Nonetheless, this gesture towards including a more culturally responsive curricula is still appreciated, and yet it's only a gesture. What's truly needed are more widespread overhauls of entire school curricula that are wholly inclusive and culturally relevant throughout all subjects and content areas. But are schools really ready to make this a reality and come to terms with the transformative power of culturally relevant curricula? No matter the powerful resistance that culturally relevant curricula experiences, it does not compare to the ultimate power it has in creating greater educational access and opportunity for marginalized students once embraced.

Educational scholars have instructed us for decades about the power of culturally relevant curricula (Banks, 2019; Gay, 2010; Ladson-Billings, 2009; Sleeter, 2012). Culturally relevant curricula are defined as "a pedagogy that empowers students intellectually, socially, emotionally, and politically by using cultural references to impart knowledge, skills, and attitudes" (Ladson-Billings, 2009, p. 20). Not to be confused with its counterpart culturally responsive teaching, which uses "the cultural knowledge, prior experiences, frames of reference, and performance styles of ethnically diverse students to make learning encounters more relevant and effective for them" (Gay, 2010, p. 31); culturally relevant or responsive curriculum has many benefits both inside and outside the classroom.

Teaching with a culturally relevant curriculum has the ability to see students' cultural differences as assets; create authentic and caring learning environments; utilize the cultural knowledge of diverse students to make learning more relevant and meaningful; increase their engagement and academic achievement; and promote positive racial identities in all students (Gay, 2010). Ultimately, it creates classroom and school environments that are committed to positively developing the *whole* student and interrupting the negative effects that the continued maintenance of dominant cultural norms has had on culturally diverse students (Ladson-Billings, 2009). Yes, culturally relevant teaching is a game-changer. It doesn't rest in the comforts of the status quo, which says only some students can succeed. It stands unapologetically alone in declaring the value of the knowledge that all students bring into the classroom and continuously finds ways to help students learn more authentically about the value of themselves and others.

One of the major aspects of a culturally relevant curriculum that makes it so effective in teaching nondominant and dominant student groups is its ties to the ultimate change-maker stance: social justice education. Social justice education seeks to "challenge, confront, and disrupt misconceptions, untruths, and stereotypes that lead to structural inequality and discrimination based on social and human differences" and to "promote critical thinking and agency for social change" (Nieto, 2010, p. 46) is the end result of culturally relevant curricula. Yes, change is the goal, not passing tests, not compliance and assimilation; but change. If you are an educator who claims to want to be effective for marginalized students, yet is unwilling to aid in empowering them to learn, grow, and change the injustices they face through education, you cannot be a culturally responsive teacher. In fact, you will be an irrelevant teacher.

Being an educator who is committed to teaching through a culturally relevant curriculum must be able to embody the characteristics of a culturally relevant teacher. We cannot continue to be satisfied with half-steps in these endeavors but must become wholly committed to building on students' strengths by growing in our cultural competence; acknowledging societal oppressions by growing in our socio-political awareness; and being the bridge that connects the outside world to the importance of academic knowledge (Byrd, 2016). To ensure the key components and inclusion of more culturally relevant and social justice-driven curricula and resources are available for use, teachers should be advocating that their school leaders provide them more opportunities to do so.

School leaders and educational institutions that train teachers need to place more significant investments in culturally responsive, culturally sustaining, and equity-based education for pre-service and in-service teachers (Jackson & Boutte, 2018). Research explains that many teachers lack high-quality (if any) exposure to ethnic studies and multicultural education in their learning opportunities and leaves them ineffective in implementing these approaches in the classroom (Jupp et al., 2019). As many teachers enter the classroom with race-evasive understandings of diversity, they effectively exacerbate inequalities in schools and reinforce the discriminatory practices upheld by the current status quo (Jupp et al., 2019). Culturally relevant curriculum promises cannot be fulfilled with educators who are not committed or competent enough to do it.

For educators committed to including a culturally relevant curriculum and schools committed to developing more culturally responsive teachers, take a look at the following strategies and suggestions for making this goal a reality:

Fostering Culturally Responsive Teachers and Schools

- Teachers can create committees or student advocacy groups to design curriculum to reflect a variety of culturally diverse histories, experiences, and languages. Consider the diversity of the local, state, national, and global populations.
- Teachers can ensure homework and other classroom materials are in multiple languages.
- Teachers can connect standard content/objectives with the daily lives of students through music or movies and other youth cultural knowledge and interests.
- School leaders can support teachers by integrating standards that align with elements of cultural pluralism and social justice.
- School leaders can provide teachers time and support in auditing teaching materials to assess whether they are inclusive of the diverse histories, perspectives, values, and beliefs of diverse peoples.
- School leaders can invest in professional development that fosters teachers' growth and development in cultural responsiveness. This can also include developing their abilities to assess bias and inequities in school practices and policies.
- School leaders can support educators in designing assessment procedures and processes to allow for multiple forms that take into account the diverse learning needs of their students (i.e., learning styles and language proficiencies, etc.). (Ebersole et al., 2016; Hilaski, 2020; Khalifa, 2018; Sleeter, 2012)

However, some teachers may not be able to do what it takes to be a culturally relevant teacher for every learner. Fear of the unknown or commitments to the status quo can hinder and halt many culturally responsive efforts (Macedo & Bartholome, 2000). We can be successful in turning the tide towards true education through the emancipatory teaching of culturally relevant practices. We can become the educators who are prepared to teach in the most culturally and linguistically diverse schools the U.S. has ever seen. We can prepare ourselves to open our minds to the possibilities of what more diverse ways of thinking and teaching can bring us in our diverse school settings. Becoming educators who can utilize culturally relevant curricula to make learning more meaningful and engaging for all students is the new goal for 21st-century teachers and schools. Not only is it the goal, but it is also the means to the end of inequitable school environments and places greater emphasis on creating learning experiences where not only some students succeed, but every student. The goal of creating equitable learning environments will be key in this accomplishment.

Creating Equitable Learning Environments

Creating more equitable environments begins with a commitment to actively engage in developing the knowledge, skills, and dispositions necessary for such a transformation. In the context of increasingly diverse schools with students from various backgrounds, with various needs, making sure the learning environments we create are equitable and that "every student has access to the curriculum, assessment, pedagogy, and challenge he or she needs based on the recognition and response to individual differences and the sociopolitical context of teaching and learning" will take careful intention and planning to do so (National Association for Multicultural Education, n.d.). Unfortunately, many schools feel as if they already have created equitable schools and brush off the need for reflective inquiry in this area. Many schools, which rely on a surface-level understanding of equality and simply treating all students the same, miss out on the transformative power of authentic equity approaches, which seek to ensure that students don't just get the same thing, but they get what they need to be academically and socially successful in school and the society at large. Consider the following scenario of two schools and their approaches to equity. As you read, think about each school's approach to equity and reflect on which school you believe will be successful in reaching its goal.

Scenario 1: Smith Elementary School (Pseudonym)

Smith Elementary School is a small, Title 1 school inside a large urban district. The student demographic makeup of the school consists mostly of students of color who hail from mostly low-income socioeconomic backgrounds. There is also a large English-learning community as many students and their families speak Spanish as their first language. The teacher demographics are similar in make-up as leadership at the school understands the importance of students having teachers in their classrooms who come from similar racial, ethnic, and linguistic backgrounds as the students. The teachers at Smith Elementary are very committed to meeting the needs of the students in their community. They often express this commitment by their belief that all students can succeed and seek to build authentic relationships with students, families, and local community members. In their teaching practices, they understand the importance of students learning collaboratively. They have created classroom environments where students learn from and teach each other with the knowledge they already have. They view teaching as a co-creative relationship in which students and teachers create and share knowledge with each other. Teachers at Smith Elementary view the content knowledge that they share with their students through a critical lens and seek to provide multiple perspectives when introducing new topics. Curriculum is culturally responsive in nature and reflects the voices and experiences of the students in the classroom and diverse peoples across the globe. Although many of the students come from low-income backgrounds, teachers hold high expectations for all learners and work collaboratively with parents to meet the educational goals set by the students and their families at the beginning of the year. Because of the strong focus on creating relationships with students and families, behavior issues are nearly non-existent. The typical hurdles that high poverty schools experience are not present at Smith due to the strong collaborative relationships among students, teachers, and families.

Scenario 2: Martin High School (Pseudonym)

Martin High School is in the same urban school district as Smith Elementary School. Although it is not a Title I school like Smith, it is a multi-racial school with student demographics that consist of Asian/Pacific Islander American, African American, Latinx/Hispanic American, and Native American students with White and Asian/Pacific Islander students making up the majority of the student population. Many of these students often came from middle or higher socioeconomic backgrounds. The teacher demographics are not reflective of the diverse student population. Many of the teachers are White and female, and the school leadership team is also majority White with a male principal and two female assistant principals. Martin High School has a strong reputation as one of the "good schools" in their urban district due to its recognized state testing record. The teachers at Martin High School are mostly veteran teachers, with the majority having more than 10 years of teaching experience. Their expertise in content knowledge led many of the teachers to see teaching as a mere technical occupation and see themselves as only needing to transfer their knowledge to their students. Not much time is spent on building relationships between teachers, students, and families, as many teachers feel that getting through the curriculum during its allotted time is what's most important. Many of the learning opportunities are based on individual forms of learning. Students are often given packets at the beginning of the week to work through, and homework is also administered in the same manner. The curriculum is often reused without revision for the changing student demographic needs, and remedial classes often fill up quickly with students who have difficulty filling out their packets quickly and quietly or those who need assistance in doing so. The overall school climate is satisfactory in the eyes of the teachers and administrators even though several students and families of color have complained about the negative racial climate of the school as slurs have been penned on bathroom stalls and racially problematic text exchanges and "blackface" videos circulate every year among students. The school leadership team often minimizes the effects of these incidents on the students and has never formally addressed any of the aforementioned incidents. They feel putting too much attention on these issues only encourages more to occur. Overall, many of the parents and students of color (particularly African American) feel as if the school staff and environment are not very welcoming to diversity as the school often boasts of its dedication to its namesake who has historical ties to oppression and disenfranchisement of marginalized groups. Past attempts for students of color to develop clubs dedicated to supporting and recognizing cultural heritage months were discouraged by the administration as they felt they would stoke racial animosity from and towards White students.

Which school do you think has a better chance of creating equitable learning environments for the diverse students they serve? Which school's approach to relationship building will create more positive results? Which approach to the curriculum will serve to meet the various needs of every student versus those that can naturally assimilate to the desires of the teacher? Which school has the ability to foster positive and inclusive learning environments that can affirm and value the cultural diversity of the students within it? In attempting to create more equitable schools, questions like these are important and can guide us in understanding which schools' approach is worth imitating and which one should be used as a cautionary tale. Ultimately, the goal is to imitate best practices that help teachers create more equitable schools. To do this, schools must be willing to rethink and reframe their beliefs about the roles of teachers, the roles of the curriculum, and the kinds of learning environments necessary to move us away from culturally unresponsive practices, which treat all students the same (while normalizing and privileging dominant norms), to more transformative ones rooted in true forms of differentiation that are able to meet the diverse needs of all of our students.

Differentiation for Real

The term differentiation in schools has been defined and executed in many different ways. It can technically be described as "the process of identifying students' individual learning strengths, needs, and interests and adapting lessons to match them" (Sparks, 2020). Unfortunately, the discourse around differentiated practices has not always been so clear-cut. The debate on the effectiveness of these practices ranges from differentiation deniers like educator James R. Delisle (2015), who claims differentiation in schools doesn't work, to differentiation advocates like Carol Ann Tomlinson (2015), who constantly sing its praises if it's done right. No matter what side of the aisle you fall on, one thing is clear: differentiated instruction's intention is to help teachers meet the diverse needs of their students. However, this discussion will not be about whether differentiated instruction is effective. This discussion assumes it is because equity depends on it. Differentiated classrooms embed the diverse learning needs of the students as standard and know that different learning needs among students are normal and not an indication of a deficit. Instead, this discussion will focus on how having a differentiated approach in our classrooms and allowing students to learn within their individual and cultural strengths can help us move away from mainstream methods which privilege only some forms of teaching and learning. Our goal is to make way for more diverse practices of teaching, learning, and instruction that make our learning environments more equitable and *successful* for all. Teachers must be willing and able to rethink best practices in creating curriculum, instructional methods, assessment techniques, and any other aspects of school that assume sameness amongst their diverse learners.

Whether teachers realize it or not, our thoughts and beliefs about teaching heavily influence how we approach instruction and our students. Many teachers believe "if I teach it and they don't learn it, the problem is not that I didn't teach it in a way that they could learn it; it's that they can't learn it." This is false. How we teach matters just as much as what we teach. More importantly, who we are teaching and the learning styles and needs of those individuals should be driving factors in helping us decide the who, what, when, and the how of classroom instruction delivery methods. So, what are your thoughts on what "good teaching" looks like?

Learning Styles. Myth or Fact?

If the debates about differentiated instruction are any indication of the lack of congruity in teaching methods among educators, the discussions surrounding the presence of learning styles will make your head spin. The 'for or against' learning styles discussion has been hotly debated for years and continues today. It has been difficult for me to reconcile the contradictions between the bodies of evidence that suggest learning styles are a "myth" (Furey, 2020; Kirshner, 2017) versus those that support the culturally responsive practice of the inclusion of learning styles or learning preferences in instruction (Banks, 2019; Gay, 2010; Ladson-Billings, 1995). For me, the heart of the matter is the battle of *whose* knowledge matters more?

I understand that the critics of learning styles say that they can't take its claims seriously because its research lacks "empirical" or "scientific" evidence to support it (Furey, 2020; Kirshner, 2017). I even understand the critics like James R. Delisle (2015) who say this kind of instruction, along with differentiated instruction, is impossible to implement in practice as teachers are ill-trained and under-resourced to do so effectively. These critiques, though well-written and good-sounding, are, in my opinion, not accurate either. These critiques are more so directed at the misinterpretation and stereotyping that accompanies the attempts to include learning styles, and the focus should stay there, not in "debunking" that learning styles even exist. Just because a theory is misunderstood or poorly practiced doesn't mean it isn't valid. Does it? Don't the decades of research on the validity of culturally responsive practices, which also include components of the effectiveness of the consideration of learning styles/preferences, count too? As conscious educators grounded in the theories and practices of culturally responsive teaching, we know learning styles matter, and we know the importance of them in our classrooms (Pritchard, 2013;

Salkind, 2008). Culturally responsive education pioneer Geneva Gay (2010) makes it clear for educators in saying, "If teachers are to do effective culturally responsive teaching, they need to understand how ethnically diverse students learn" (p. 174).

However, it must be clear that although there are culturally specific learning styles, not all students within a particular ethnic or cultural group will display those characteristics at all times, if at all. No cultural group is a monolith. Instead of oversimplifying learning styles and running the risk of creating harmful and false stereotypes about student groups, "learning styles should be seen as tools for improving the school achievement of Latino, Native, Asian, and African American students by creating more *cultural congruity* in teaching-learning processes" (Gay, 2010, p. 174). By no means are students to be separated or segregated based on these characteristics, and the consideration of learning styles should only be used to help make learning encounters more relevant and equitable by utilizing the natural learning strengths of our students.

This understanding is important because our classrooms were traditionally designed to serve as spaces that reinforce the status quo of the dominant cultural norms and beliefs of White, male, middle-class, English speaking, heteronormative, and conservative Christian values (Anderson, 1988; Tyack, 1984). In the multiracial, multilingual schools of today, the continued adherence to these norms, knowingly or unknowingly, has devastating consequences for the students who think, act, and believe outside these norms. If our goal is more equitable classrooms and schools, we must be open to reorganizing them for the benefit of all. In doing so, we must be willing to create learning spaces that allow African American students to engage in the communal, performative, or rhythmic preferences they exhibit when interacting at home or with friends (Boykin et al., 2004). We must be willing to provide the cooperative learning opportunities that many African/Black American, some Asian American, and Latinx/Hispanic students thrive on while also maintaining the independent learning options of many White and certain Asian American students need without continuing to prioritize these styles as the expected norm for all (Tong, 1978). Creating learning spaces where all student's individual learning strengths and needs are recognized and valued reduces the underachievement of nondominant student groups and creates the true equity we wish to see in our classrooms and schools (Banks, 2019; Gay, 2010).

Equitable classrooms are designed for the success of every learner. From how teachers choose curriculum to how they assess student knowledge of content to where students are allowed to work, every aspect of our classrooms and instruction must be carefully considered to ensure we are not privileging some learning modes over others. With so many learning and teaching styles, teachers may wonder how they will discover these styles and how to accommodate them. As stated in earlier chapters, we must get to know our students and their families and understand their true educational values, beliefs, and goals through intentional and authentic relationship-building efforts.

At the beginning of the school year, relationship and rapport building should be a top priority before the introduction of any formal learning experience. Our classrooms should be viewed as communities, and these communities should be created with the interests and needs of the students and families it was designed to serve. Developing collaborative relationships between students and their families will provide teachers with vital information about student learning preferences and learning goals in regards to their past and present learning experiences. In a perfect world, we would be able to have one-on-one interviews with each student and family to find out the details of these components. Unfortunately, we do not live in a perfect world, and teachers do not have the time to sit with every student and family before the school year begins. However, conducting learning surveys before the start of school can be a great alternative to obtain this vital information while developing positive communication patterns with students and their families.

Student surveys can ask questions such as:

1. What are your favorite subjects?
2. What are your favorite books/comics?
3. Do you enjoy video games? If so, which ones do you like to play?
4. Do you prefer to work in a group or independently?
5. Where do you study at home? Is it comfortable? If not, what would be your ideal study space?
6. Would you rather read a famous person's biography or watch a movie about their life?
7. How would you prefer to show what you know? In a written report? In a play you acted out? In a musical performance or spoken word session? In an art project or 3D model? Using technology by creating a video, podcast, etc? Or something else?

Parent/Guardian/Family surveys can have questions such as:

1. What are your child's learning strengths? Struggles?
2. In what language does your family prefer to receive information?
3. What educational goals do you have for your child?
4. What past educational hurdles has your child overcome?
5. How do you teach your child a new skill/task?
6. What help will you need to support your child's learning?
7. In what ways do you prefer to show support for your child's learning? By volunteering at school? By helping with homework?

Any of these questions will be a great start in guiding teachers to create learning environments that are inclusive of the diverse needs of their students. With this information, curriculum planning can more easily integrate diverse identities, histories, and experiences. Asking these questions of students and families shows a commitment to relationship-building and adapting the school environment to fit the needs of the student. Methods of assessment or checking for understanding can also be done in differentiated ways based on the learning profiles of our students. Instead of mid-week pop quizzes, students can choose to work in small groups to create a quick video presentation in a virtual learning platform of their choice. Likewise, a friendly game of Jeopardy can be played to see which students need more engagement with the new material. The reteaching of these concepts can now be offered by providing a variety of media, board work, group work, and seat work (The Derek Bok Center for Teaching and Learning, n.d.) Final assessments can also take into consideration the learning styles of students by varying between paper/pencil multiple choice exams and options that include art projects, performances, or a demonstration of their choice (Gibson, 2020). The point is to provide every student with as many ways to learn and grow through their strengths, to create learning environments that value the diverse learning styles of every student, and to see their learning preferences as just as valuable as others. This is the epitome of an equitable learning environment.

Creating equitable learning spaces for our diverse students doesn't have to be difficult. If we value the diversity of our students, these accommodations will become second nature. We will no longer see the differentiation needed to create these environments as hassles, but instead as essential best practices in helping every student succeed. Questioning the equity present in our learning environments is the first step in this process. We must ask ourselves: Have I created a learning space that values what every student brings to the table or only some? Do I even believe in the value of the diverse learning styles my students bring with them into the classroom? If you don't believe and can't see the value, what are you willing to do to change that?

In truth, we teach what we believe. If we believe differences in learning are deficits, we will create spaces of marginalization and underachievement. If we believe differences are a part of the learning process and value the differences within ourselves and our students, we help students embrace the diversity within themselves and accept the diversity of others.

Teachers and Students as Co-Collaborators

I first learned about the power of collaborative teaching in a kindergarten classroom during an instructional unit on Texas Leaders. We were to focus on the contributions of famed Texas "heroes," Stephen F. Austin and Jose Antonio Navarjo. With all due respect to curriculum writers and Texas history buffs at large, this was some dull (and whitewashed) stuff. Not only that, but to isolate these two individuals as the only "heroes" in Texas history perpetuates the erasure of groups of color in these retellings and the marginalization, enslavement, genocide, and land theft that was necessary in creating the conditions for their "heroic" contributions. For teachers who are responsible for exposing students to all genres of knowledge, the focus on the history of "dead White men" or even the people of color who assisted them can be amongst the most challenging tasks in today's multiracial schools.

The predetermined methods in which these lessons are typically taught involve individualized, boring, decontextualized textbooks, outdated or biased videos, worksheets, and other paper/pencil activities that bore students to death and do not allow for creativity or an in-depth understanding of the historical importance of not only these two individuals, but how their contributions affected others. Collaborative teaching hopes to change that. When teachers provide students with the opportunity to become co-collaborators who are involved in their own learning process, they experience multiple academic and social-emotional benefits when taking charge of their learning in this manner (Villa et al., 2011). In a co-collaborative environment, the natural tendency for students to shine as designers, decision-makers, and critical thinkers proves beneficial to their self-esteem and academic potential.

Collaborative teaching can be described as "a set of teaching and learning strategies promoting student collaboration in small groups (two to five students) in order to optimize their own and each other's learning" (Johnson & Johnson, 1999). It may also be described as *cooperative learning*, which is just another way of describing the manner in which student learning is conducted in groups (Slavin, 2014). Both terms are sometimes used interchangeably; however, they serve the same purpose because, "Cooperation, collaboration, and community are prominent themes, techniques, and goals in educating marginalized Latino, Native, African, and Asian American students" (Gay, 2010, p. 187). The discussion about these techniques will be another tool to aid teachers in creating learning environments that are responsive to the needs of their diverse learners resulting in more positive and equitable school outcomes.

Academically, collaborative learning has been said to increase the overall achievement of students due to its emphasis on peer tutoring, partner learning, and reciprocal teaching" (Villa, 2011). This happens because students must increase their own mastery of the desired content in order to teach it to their classmates. Research has revealed that these tutor/tutee relationships, inherent in collaborative working conditions, are beneficial for all students. Age limits, special education, nor learning challenges should hinder teachers from creating these opportunities for students. Every learner can participate and receive educational and social benefits from either role. It also increases students' motivation to learn new content as every learner can be more fully engaged as they now have a responsibility to teach it (Borich, 2015).

Socially, collaborative learning helps students practice much-needed communication skills necessary for school and real-life experiences. Students who have the opportunity to serve as teachers to their fellow classmates have reported greater self-esteem, self-determination, and stronger friendships within these group dynamics (Pathak & Entratat, 2012; Villa, 2011). Teachers and students also increase the rapport in their relationships because students feel trusted and expected to perform at higher levels. The typical one-sided, all-knowing teacher at the front of the room experience can transition to teacher as the facilitator as students are now allowed to take on more responsibility for their learning outcomes. However, as beneficial as collaborative learning can be, it does come with some caution, as getting any group of students to work together can present some challenges. No teacher should jump into creating these collaborative learning environments without first understanding the potential pitfalls and considerations in making these experiences as successful as possible.

As mentioned before, the power of collaborative learning and co-collaborative partnerships between teachers and students was realized during my own teaching and growing experience. Cooperative groups are effective teaching for all learners if done right. As most young learners, my students were never shy about communicating their likes or dislikes in the classroom setting or classroom environment. This is not conducive to a positive group experience. When putting students in groups, we want to not only make sure they are academically beneficial, but also productive in problem-solving and cooperative learning. Often when students are placed in groups without significant prior practice in this arena, they do "not pay attention to others" opinions, interrupt them, and reject alternative suggestions without justification" (Le et al., 2018). This is not ideal.

To ensure students can work together and solve any problems independently, teachers should first help students understand the importance of working together. Practicing often with guidance in team building, trust-building, conflict management, and active listening skills will be key in successfully turning loose your students to work among themselves (Burns, 2016). Also, co-creating expectations for how students think group members should participate will ensure that all students have an opportunity to voice their needs within the group while making decisions collaboratively on how to meet those requirements. Jotting down community agreements will help students stay on target while working, as these can be displayed around the classroom for every group to reference.

Another issue that often harms the collaborative learning environments we seek to create is the presence of "free riding." Free riders are those students (or colleagues) that are more than happy to allow everyone in the group to carry the workload for them. This is also problematic. To prevent this, teachers can create small groups of 3-4 students so that all work can easily be shouldered by every group member. They can also create team roles so that all students have specific tasks that they are responsible for. Teachers may also consider creating a peer-evaluation system to ensure students feel the sting of accountability. If students know they will be assessed on their contributions, they may be more inclined to contribute (Burns, 2016). In the end, preparing and planning for the ups and downs in any collaborative opportunity will be key to its success. Remember, no positive and effective group dynamics will happen overnight. Be sure to not only give your students time to practice and make mistakes, but give yourself the leniency to do so as well.

For my kinders, tackling the history of Texas leaders became less of a chore and more of a time-traveling mystery within these cooperative groups. The key to the success of these co-collaborative opportunities was that I was not the only source of knowledge, and I did not make all the decisions. Whew! Not only was this a great relief for me, but also, I was able to see the inherent strengths of many of my five- and six-year-olds who were excellent at formulating questions, posing solutions, and using digital resources to get the answers they were looking for. My majority role as facilitator was to make sure we stayed on topic and focused on the content. In the end, my kinders were able to discover not only who Stephen F. Austin and Jose Antonio Navarro were, but through the multiple perspectives approach inherent in all of my lessons, they were also able to make connections and understand how the demographics of Texas changed between Stephen F. Austin's arrival and today. Yes, we did discuss the land theft of Native and Indigenous peoples in Texas. Yes, we did discuss the enslaved African men, women, and children who accompanied the Old Three Hundred. Yes, we talked about the fights that erupted in the disputes to maintain the institution of slavery on behalf of Texas "patriots" as a result (Gordon-Reed, 2021). And most importantly, my students were able to excitedly write about and share the most interesting facts they learned about this unit.

Reflect on the following considerations in creating your cooperative learning environments by examining these characteristics of cooperative learning groups. Consider the following criteria when establishing your student groups:

- Create a learning environment that values group cooperation even outside of learning tasks.
- Allow learners to think for themselves.
- Consist of 3-6 members.
- Allow the teacher to be the facilitator. Teachers can intervene at critical moments, but students should be able to interact with new learning on their own.
- Tasks should be pre-planned, timed, and completed in stages.
- Tasks should be complex and require multiple abilities to accomplish.
- Change group members often so that all students have a chance to work with different people.
- Assign roles to each member of the group to ensure participation, ownership, and accountability. Roles may include: summarizer, fact-checker, researcher, supply runner, recorder, supporter, or observer/troubleshooter (Borich, 2015).

For a culturally responsive classroom environment to be successful, collaborative learning opportunities are key as they not only contribute to academic success, they help students bridge those gaps in conflicts that may arise when working with those different from themselves. A key practice in this is making sure teachers establish an environment that respects all students and ideas. Remember, teachers are the models. If teachers show respect for different ways of thinking, acting, and believing, students will too.

There are many reasons why integrating co-collaborative learning opportunities for our students should be implemented at large. From its fostering of independent, confident, and self-motivated students; to its effectiveness in obtaining those 21st-century learning goals of communication and generosity (Villa, 2011); whether it's cooperative or collaborative teaching, no school should be considered effective without it. My kinders took their responsibility of teaching themselves and each other about Texas history very seriously. As we researched and explored the topic together, they were able to pose questions and guide their learning in ways I could not have come up with on my own. Most importantly, the key to co-collaboration with our students is trust. My students trusted that I was going to hold them accountable for high levels of learning while I trusted them to learn all they could and work together while doing so. However, no high levels of learning can occur without high expectations from the students and the teacher.

Fostering High Expectations for Every Student

In *The Autobiography of Malcolm X* (1964), X recollects the story of the first time he realized his "otherness" in being the only Black student in his class. He recalls the time in the seventh grade when he was asked by his teacher, Mr. Ostrowski, what he wanted to be when he grew up. Malcolm, being the top student in his class, replied that he wanted to be a lawyer. To Malcolm's shock and dismay, his teacher explained that his desire was an unrealistic aspiration and an impossible one due to the fact that Malcolm was a "n*****." This was a painful realization for Malcolm as this teacher was someone he actually liked, and his opinion made an unforgettable impression on him. This pivotal moment in his life put an outgoing and remarkable student on a path of social withdrawal and academic tediousness that eventually led to his departure from that Michigan school the following year. As an adult, Malcolm X reflected on how Mr. Ostrowski's words discouraged him from pursuing his dream of becoming a successful lawyer. Thankfully, Malcolm X was also able to see how not becoming a lawyer enabled him to become something else. As history tells it, he was able to become something even greater. However, the biases exhibited by his teacher are not uncommon and still relevant today. Many adults can reflect back to the teachers who had the influence to "make or break" what path they pursued. Although we are not all called to be prolific civil rights activists, we are *all* called to greatness in our own right. How and when that greatness manifests can very well depend on the encouragement and expectations of the educators in front of us.

Teacher expectations matter. According to research, "Teachers are the single most important in-school factor that affects student achievement" (Education Commission of the States, 2012). Teacher expectations set the tone for students to succeed or fail in school. These teacher expectations can be described as "ideas teachers hold about the potential achievement of students" (Rubie-Davies, 2015). Another way to look at it could be that what teachers think or believe about students and their potential or ability plays a huge part in determining the outcomes of students' academic or behavioral performance. If a teacher believes and enforces practices that support students' success, students will be successful. If a teacher doesn't believe and enforce successful practices, the opposite will be true. That's powerful stuff!

Much research has been conducted about the power of teacher expectations, and it's been made clear that the thoughts and beliefs of educators can act as a self-fulfilling prophecy when it comes to student achievement (de Boer et al., 2018; Lynch, 2020). The legendary research of Rosenthal and Jacobson (1968) coined this interaction the *Pygmalion Effect* and documented its harmful effects on students as it determines the kinds of interactions teachers have with students and the high-quality or lack of learning experiences they provide in the classroom.

Where do these expectations come from? How do they form? Sadly, many teachers base these expectations on things such as race, gender, socioeconomic status, ableness, language proficiency, and other student characteristics that are out of students' control (Timmermans et al., 2015). Teachers who carry deficit beliefs about diverse students and their families are said to exhibit negative teacher expectations, which result in providing less wait time for students, calling on students less often, providing less help, spending less time listening to, providing less challenging work, and ignoring students who they believe are less capable of high levels of achievement (Hughes et al., 2005; Tenenbaum & Ruck, 2007). In the reverse, teachers who carry positive expectations about students provide them with more praise, more challenging work, more help, and even call on them more often than those they do not (Jussim et al., 1996). As a whole, low-income and students of color are viewed with lower expectations than White, middle, or upper-class students. Negative teacher expectations contribute greatly to the disparities we see in achievement rates and discipline outcomes of already marginalized students (Education Commission of the States, 2012). Frankly, I didn't need research to tell me this much is true. My own experiences as a young, Black, female student reflected many of these characteristics, and my story is unfortunately eerily similar to other students of color, particularly Black females, in today's classrooms and schools.

This One's Personal

The following is an adapted excerpt from an article I published in The Lighthouse Almanac Journal (Grice, 2021).

Let me be perfectly honest; math is *not* my jam. However, my aversion to all things mathematical didn't begin in the early grades, as I felt perfectly capable and happy to perform and engage in mathematical scenarios in elementary school. Instead, this uneasy and uncomfortable feeling about math did not develop until my middle and high school years. My aversion to math mostly stems from the way math concepts were presented to me, and the teachers who presented them. In short, my mathematical career in school looked a lot like this: If I liked the teacher, I did well; if I didn't, I did poorly. In the same fashion, if I felt like the teacher liked me, I did well; if not…you get the picture.

One may think that my experiences as a math student were atypical or only reflective of my willingness to learn or general math ability. After all, we all have come to believe the idea that some people are "math people," and some aren't (Kimball et al., 2013). This false assumption about my inherent genetic math inability helped me to sleep at night, too. Unfortunately, many students perform poorly in certain subjects not because they are "not good" at them, but their success or failure ultimately rested on the effectiveness of the teacher instructing them and the relationship between that instructor and themselves (Booker & Lim, 2018). As an African American female student, my relationships with many of my former math teachers seemed volatile at most and indifferent at best. It wasn't until I became an educator that I realized these negative experiences weren't wholly the result of my deficiencies; they were also due to the educational neglect of those in charge of my instruction.

For myself and many young, adolescent African American girls, the relationship with their math instructors is a significant factor in their math success; the presence of positive, welcoming, and inclusive classroom environments are essential for high-level math achievement (Diemer et al., 2016). A positive teacher-student relationship is vital to ALL students' success, but for students of color, it's even more critical. For African American girls in the math classroom, experiencing negative, discriminatory, and unresponsive classroom environments (and teachers) often leads to disengagement, behavior problems, and academic underachievement (Morton, 2014). Unfortunately, many of my past instructors missed the memo on building positive classroom environments and maintaining high expectations for all students. However, today's social media savvy and professional development overloaded teachers have fewer excuses for this lack of best practices knowledge. If teachers want to create more math-minded and successful African American math students, they must assess their expectations of those students and make adjustments as needed.

However, developing high expectations of teachers with diverse students will not only require them to assess what they know about their students' abilities but also what they believe about them too. It is critical that educators understand that "a teacher's ideology or mindset is inextricably linked to his or her practice in the classroom. Teacher beliefs are powerful determinants for how they perform in the classroom" (Hill-Jackson & Stafford, p. xvii, 2017). Teachers need to have ample opportunity to examine how their beliefs about racial, ethnic, socioeconomic, gender, or religious differences in students influence their beliefs about how a good student looks, acts, sounds, and thinks. They need to check their assumptions about their diverse students' capabilities, as many teachers hold deficit views specifically about African American students and their readiness to perform high-level tasks and operations (Davis & Martin, 2018). As a result, those students, who initially may have felt competent and capable, sense their teacher's apathy or lack of care regarding their academic success. They then enter into a self-fulfilling prophecy and perform according to the standards and expectations established consciously and subconsciously by the teacher (Jett, 2013). Just as I performed poorly for teachers I deemed unresponsive and uncaring, many of our students today are doing the same. Critical self-reflection among educators is essential in helping teachers become conscious of their deeply-held beliefs about diverse students and how those beliefs shape their teaching practices (Gooden & Dantley, 2021; Grice, 2019). This process is essential in overturning harmful classroom practices which exclude and withhold high-quality learning experiences and replace them with positive, supportive, expectant, and inclusive ones.

Where Do We Go from Here?

The good news is teachers can interrupt this cycle of low expectations. Teachers can change the student outcomes for underachieving students and begin to create pathways toward success. But first, we must change what we think so that our actions will follow. As educational scholars Valerie Hill-Jackson and Delia Stafford (2017) stated:

> If a teacher believes that all students can learn, and these learners have the potential to be successful, s/he will move heaven and earth to ensure that the learners on his or her watch will experience academic success. However, if a teacher feels in his or her heart that there is no hope for learners, then he or she is less likely to implement the practices to support student learning. (p. xvii)

Let's be the believers for our most marginalized students and put in the work to move heaven and earth for greater access to the learning, experiences, and opportunities they deserve. For those ready for the challenge, there are several principles educators can adhere to in order to alter their low expectations of their most marginalized students. These principles are more aligned with higher expectations which can increase student achievement and usher in those high-quality learning experiences every student needs and wants.

- **Maintain high expectations for all students regardless of social identity characteristics.** Every student has something special to offer the world. While in school, every student should be provided with an environment that expects nothing less than that, and works diligently to provide diverse learning experiences that help them become empowered and engaged citizens in the world. Gender, race, sexual orientation, first language, socioeconomic status, nor ableness determines a student's worth.
- **Reflect on your explicit/implicit biases.** As educators who have been socialized in a racialized and racist society, no one is exempt from these critical reflections. Implicit or explicit bias; negative unconscious or conscious beliefs we have about those different from ourselves are problematic and need to be consciously interrupted. The Harvard Implicit Bias Test (https://implicit.harvard.edu/implicit/takeatest.html) can be used as a great indicator tool to help teachers figure out where to start in this process. Reflecting on our deeply held beliefs about those who are different from us can help pinpoint problematic viewpoints and stereotypes about diverse groups of people. Once identified, it will be even more important to engage in the work necessary to replace those negative understandings with ones that are more accurate, complete, and positive about cultural or linguistic diversity.
- **Grow your knowledge in culturally responsive practices.** Teachers' knowledge of students' culture is critical in this endeavor as they must understand the histories,

perspectives, values, beliefs, and customs of culturally diverse students. Culture counts, and it is a significant factor in creating culturally responsive learning environments for all students. With this knowledge, teachers will no longer rely on assumptions about student motivations or behaviors because they will know who their students are and what they need to succeed. In turn, they can use that knowledge to create more relevant, meaningful, and positive learning environments for all students (Gay, 2010).

- **Make academically challenging curricula non-negotiable.** Every student wants to succeed. Yes, *every* student. No student begins their educational careers thinking they will fail, so let's ensure that all students know they can succeed and that teachers are committed to doing all they can to help them. Getting rid of tracking and other practices that divide students into groups according to "achievers" and "underachievers" need to be abolished. All students should be given access to high-quality and rigorous curriculum, and all teachers should expose students to high-level questioning and higher-order thinking processes.
- **Accept that every teacher will not be a good teacher and dispose of them accordingly.** Too much leeway is given to ineffective teachers. For some, a lack of support is at play, and an opportunity to develop skills that they lack will suffice. For others, a career in teaching should never have been a choice, and their time in the classroom should be cut short. Unfortunately, many administrators pass these "lemons" around year after year, hoping they will quit. Meanwhile, these "educators" sit back at their desks and collect a check while another generation of students receives a subpar education. Rinse, repeat. Enough is enough. Educational pioneer Martin Haberman's (1995) research on what he called *Star Teachers* makes it clear that training can only do so much for some educators. According to Haberman, Star Teachers are more than good at passing exit

exams and understanding the technical application of content knowledge; they also have the relational dispositions needed to be effective for diverse students. They can not only teach the standards, but they can also inspire hope, motivate, encourage, uplift, empower, and educate all students. They see the potential in all learners, and they have the patience to see it come to fruition. In short, Star Teachers are born. If school leaders and invested stakeholders want to see improvements in classrooms, they must invest in recruiting teachers who can pass tests *and* demonstrate commitment to equity and high achievement for all students.

Ultimately, teachers have the power to reverse the trends of underachievement for their culturally diverse students (National Assessment of Educational Progress, 2019). With the help of persistent teachers having high expectations for all students, teachers can help their so-called "at-risk" students flourish in the classroom (Minor, 2016). Perhaps, if I had educators who expected the best out of me during my secondary career, my math aversions of today could have been avoided. Thankfully, there is still hope for diverse students in the classrooms of today.

Hopefully, the underrepresentation of people of color in STEM fields can be reversed as teachers begin to recognize and cultivate the math genius in ALL students (Jett, 2013). Hopefully, the educators in today's multiracial schools know that every student deserves the opportunity to feel welcomed, valued, and inspired by their educational experiences. The goal is for the current rates of underachievement among Black, Latinx, and Native American, and low-income students to become a thing of the past as education reform moves in the direction that best fits the needs of all students, not just the ones society says is worthy of achievement.

Questions for Reflection

1. Culturally relevant pedagogy and culturally responsive teaching are similar terms with similar goals and meanings. Reflect on the differences/nuances of each term.
2. Among the strategies discussed in this chapter to help teachers incorporate culturally relevant curriculum, which ones do you feel are most important? Why?
3. Creating equity in schools must begin with a commitment to increase equitable opportunities for all students. Has your school leadership team established a commitment towards racial equity? Why or why not?
4. What elements of being an effective educator for diverse students will be more difficult for you? Why or why not?

5. INCLUDING ALL STUDENTS

 "Power is the ability not just to tell the story of another person, but to make it the definitive story of that person. Who decides which stories are told, who tells them, when are they told, and how are they told are all part of this power."

— CHIMAMANDA NGOZI ADICHIE

Reading is a favorite past-time for many people. Many people enjoy books because they add value and meaning to their lives. However, reading is not only used for enjoyment and recreation, it's also an essential skill to all levels of learning and functioning in our society. Being literate in today's 21st-century world is critical to opening many doors of success and social and economic upward mobility. However, as powerful as literature is in the education of students, are schools really meeting the literacy needs of all diverse students? Sadly, research shows that low-income students have lower levels of reading achievement than their upper/middle class counterparts (NCES, 2017a), which means the answer is "no." Black, Latinx, and Native American students also perform at lower levels in their reading achievement than their White and certain Asian counterparts (NCES, 2017a). This longstanding issue deserves a remedy.

Although there are many factors that contribute to student underachievement such as poverty, access to quality healthcare, lack of early reading interventions at home, and the quality of the curriculum and instruction at school, this section focuses on one of the most influential components and the one we can control—the teacher. Just as the quality of the educator, their instruction, and the materials they use can have a significant impact on the achievement levels of students, they can have an impact on student literacy skills too. In reference to those materials, although our classrooms are filled with students from many racially, ethnically, linguistically, socioeconomically, ability, and religiously diverse backgrounds, the books we often choose to teach these students are not. This practice begins during pre-service years as many educator preparation programs lack courses in multicultural education (Williams & Tehia, 2019). As a result, novice educators replicate the teaching practices that they were exposed to in school which also lacked a foundation in understanding multiculturalism. Additionally, not only are pre-service teachers selecting texts with predominantly White characters for use with diverse students, but in-service teachers continue to do so as well (Buchanan & Fox, 2019). It's time to break this cycle. It's time to reconsider the materials that we are using to teach and evaluate them for their ability to be effective for the students we educate. It's time to be more intentional and more inclusive with our curriculum choices. It's time to create classrooms that not only embrace, empower, and educate, but ones that also include all students as well.

An inclusive environment seeks to elevate historically marginalized and silenced voices. It also welcomes diverse sources of knowledge and aims to dismantle the assumption of superiority of dominant norms and beliefs in education. An inclusive environment values diversity and sees it as a strength, not a problem. This kind of environment makes sure that all students see accurate and positive representations of themselves and others in their learning environments. Because research tells us that students' racial identities have direct correlations to their academic achievement (Carter, 2008) and students in identity-safe classrooms perform better on standardized tests than those who are not (Cohn-Vargas, 2015), teachers must become equipped to create identity-safe and affirming classrooms for all students. Much of which will come from providing windows into the lives of those who are different and mirrors that reflect the experiences in our individual students' lives.

Renowned educator, Dr. Rudine Sims Bishop, urges teachers to expose ALL children to diverse books as "mirrors, windows, and sliding glass doors" (Sims Bishop, 1990). The sentiment behind this statement reflects the understanding that all students need learning experiences that they can identify with. Students are more connected to lessons they can see themselves in and relate to. In other words, this approach allows students to learn about other people and cultures and become more understanding of the diversity within themselves and in the world. Unfortunately, many classroom book shelves are filled with books that not only do not represent the students in our classrooms, but also paint stereotypical, inaccurate, or harmful depictions of them, if they are included at all. The common practice of stereotyping or making invisible marginalized groups and people in children's literature is getting much deserved push back as calls to "interrupt the text" make it clear that teachers and students not only want to see themselves represented in the books they read in school, but they deserve it! A teacher's ability to utilize a 'windows and mirror' approach creates the pathway for the authentic inclusion of the diverse texts all students need.

Utilizing Mirrors and Windows

One of the reasons I loved teaching kindergarten so much was the level of growth one could witness in the academic and social development of their students. When many kinders first arrive in school, they are often timid and unsure of themselves and their abilities. For many of them, my classroom was their first experience with formal instruction. It was my job to ensure a firm foundation for all future learning experiences and help students develop a love for learning in the process. I took this responsibility seriously and strived to provide learning experiences that were fun, engaging, and culturally relevant even before the term was trending. Creating such an atmosphere could be challenging at times, as some students came into kindergarten with prior experiences in high-quality preschool programs and others did not. Those who did usually approached the new learning opportunities with excitement and determination. Those with less prior experiences could show disinterest or refusal to engage in unfamiliar practices. For one of my students who we'll call Ryan, his lack of experience with formal reading instruction left him feeling less than confident in his beginning reading skills. To engage Ryan, I had to get a little creative and think outside of the campus mandated curriculum guide. For him, cultural relevance was essential and representation mattered tremendously. As a young African American boy, he needed "mirrors" in his reading instruction to help make the connections to the new literacy skills he needed. The scholarship surrounding multicultural children's literature and the effectiveness of providing "mirrors, windows, and sliding glass doors" has been well-documented and established by many researchers (Braden & Rodriguez, 2016; Sims Bishop, 1990; Style, 1996). As the student populations across many campuses continue to see disparities in teacher and student demographics (NCES, 2019), every educator must be equipped with knowledge and skills needed to provide these relevant reading experiences for all of their diverse students. We can't continue to rest in the comfort of only sharing our favorite stories; we must be knowledgeable enough to include the stories of others as well.

The Cooperative Children's Book Center (CCBC) is an organization that works to inventory, review, and research available children's literature in the publishing world. In collaboration with the CCBC, artists David Huyck and Sarah Park Dahlen created a graphic that puts the topic of "mirrors and windows" into complete perspective.

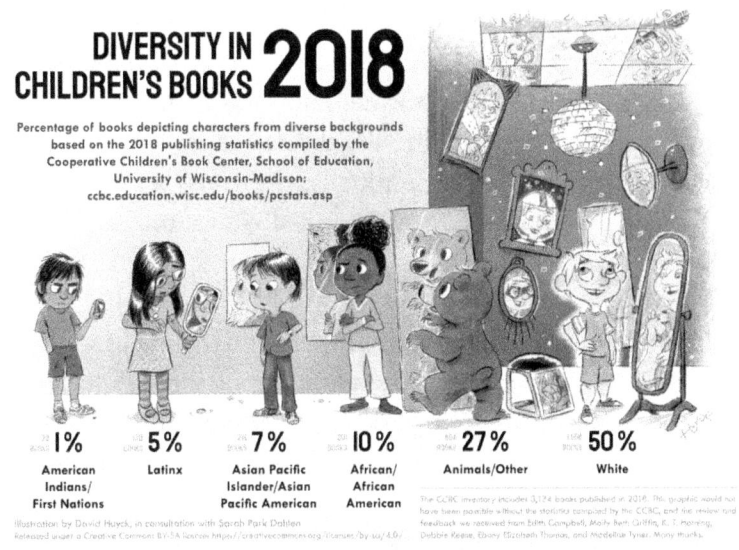

Figure 2. Diversity in Children's Books 2018

This image serves as an uncomfortable reminder that although we may have the best intentions to teach high-quality curricula, we may only be reinforcing the hegemony of whiteness in these attempts (Braden & Rodriguez, 2016). Overall, Black, Latinx, Native/Indigenous, and Asian/Pacific Islander American students are less often presented with opportunities to see authentic, accurate, or positive representations of themselves and their experiences in literature (Reading is Fundamental, 2015). To compound this issue, when they do encounter books with seemingly authentic representations, they are often filled with negative biases and stereotypes which reinforce damaging dominant narratives about diverse groups (Tschida et al., 2014).

This disparity is damaging in two ways. On one hand, diverse students do not get to develop the positive self-identities that diverse literature can help them create (Braden & Rodriguez, 2016). One the other hand, White students who see more than enough mirrors of themselves on screen and in books "will grow up with an exaggerated sense of their own importance and value in the world—a dangerous ethnocentrism" (Bishop Sims, 1990, p. x). One allows students to become invisible and feel invalidated and unimportant; the other projects a false sense of superiority and universality that can keep them from understanding and valuing the diverse experiences of others. If teachers are not aware of these pitfalls, they miss an opportunity to provide every student with a well-rounded education. As Emily Style (1996) puts it:

> If the student is understood as occupying a dwelling of self, education needs to enable the student to look through window frames in order to see the realities of others and into mirrors in order to see her/his own reality reflected. Knowledge of both types of framing is basic to a balanced education which is committed to affirming the essential dialectic between the self and the world. In other words, education engages us in "the great conversation" between various frames of reference. (p. 1)

Teachers must find this balance by diversifying their book selections and being skilled in recognizing bias and stereotypes when they inevitably present themselves. To increase the opportunities for our students to interact and learn from diverse texts, we must have a variety of sources to pull from. Below you will find an extensive list of websites and publishers who can help us create those diverse bookshelves all of our students deserve. This list is by no means exhaustive, but will get you on the right track in diversifying your bookshelf!

Building a Diverse Bookshelf

Africa Access Review
http://africaaccessreview.org/

The Brown Bookshelf
http://thebrownbookshelf.com/

The Dark Fantastic
http://thedarkfantastic.blogspot.com/

American Indians in Children's Literature
http://americanindiansinchildrensliterature.blogspot.com/

A Critical Bibliography of North American Indian for K-12
https://eric.ed.gov/?id=ED432424

Teacher and Librarian Resources for Native American Children's and YA
Books via Cynthia Leitich Smith
https://cynthialeitichsmith.com/lit-resources/read/diversity/native-am/teaching/native_resources/

Talk Story
talkstorytogether.org/

Bilingual Books
https://www.languagelizard.com/

Disability in Kidlit
http://disabilityinkidlit.wordpress.com/

SLJ's Islam in the Classroom
http://www.slj.com/2013/05/resources/islam-in-the-classroom/

Association of Jewish Libraries
https://jewishlibraries.org/index.php

Jewish Book Council
https://www.jewishbookcouncil.org/

ALA's Rainbow List
http://glbtrt.ala.org/rainbowbooks/archives/1103

Great Gay Teen Books
http://www.alexsanchez.com/gay_teen_books.htm

I'm Queer I'm Here, What the Hell Do I Read?
http://www.leewind.org/

Colorin Colorado
http://www.colorincolorado.org/

Latin@s in Kid Lit
http://latinosinkidlit.com/

Mamiverse Books
http://mamiverse.com/mamiverse-books/

Diversity in YA
http://diversityinya.tumblr.com/

Elizabeth Bluemle's a World Full of Color
http://www.librarything.com/profile/shelftalker

The Guardian: List of 50 Best Culturally Diverse Children's Books
http://www.theguardian.com/childrens-books-site/2014/oct/13/50-best-culturally-diverse-childrens-books?CMP=twt_gu

I'm Your Neighbor
http://www.imyourneighborbooks.org/

The Pirate Tree
http://www.thepiratetree.com/

Reading in Color
http://blackteensread2.blogspot.com/

Rich in Color
http://richincolor.com/

SLJ: Betsy Bird's Casual Diversity Book List
http://blogs.slj.com/afuse8production/2014/05/12/we-need-diverse-books-but-are-we-willing-to-discuss-them-with-our-kids/#_

SLJ's Culturally Diverse Book List
http://www.slj.com/2014/05/diversity/culturally-diverse-books-selected-by-sljs-review-editors/#_

Evaluating Bias in Books

After we've discovered the resources we will utilize to increase our diverse book selection, we must also work to understand whether the books we've selected will cause more harm than good. Many children's books present harmful stereotypes about gender, class, and race. Many of the biases we see in our books either promote stereotypes such as Latinx men portrayed as lazy or wearing oversized sombreros. Muslims may be portrayed as only being Arab. Black men may be portrayed as gang members, oversexed, or underemployed; and people with disabilities are not independent or should be pitied, just to name a few (Derman-Sparks, 2016).

On the other hand, many groups are simply rendered invisible as there are fewer quality depictions of families in rural areas, blue-collar workers, families with two dads or two moms, families with single mothers or fathers, homeless families, and families with an incarcerated parent (Derman-Sparks, 2016). These negative narratives of diverse people are dangerous and send messages to students that some people are valuable and others are not. Many of the societal ills we continue to see in the form of hate crimes and discriminatory policies are the result of the negative and inaccurate messages we have internalized about the value of ourselves and others. We must be skilled in finding appropriate texts to meet the needs of our diverse students and also analyzing them for bias and stereotypes.

The following suggestions are taken from *Ten Quick Ways to Analyze Children's Books for Sexism and Racism* by Derman-Sparks & A.B.C. Task Force (2013). Please use these tips as a guide in helping you determine the appropriateness of the selected texts you have chosen for your students. When looking for multicultural texts, check to see if:

- Stereotypes are present which give an oversimplified generalization of a group, race, or sex.
- Characters of color only experience success when exhibiting behaviors that resemble "whiteness."
- Problems faced by marginalized people are only solved by "good" or benevolent White characters.
- Marginalized characters are seen only in traditional or ceremonial cultural "costumes."
- White characters are exclusively the heroes, making all the decisions, or in leadership positions.
- The standards of beauty portrayed only show women or girls who are thin, have long hair, or are fair or light-skinned.
- The author is an insider or outsider of the story. For example, is the author a member of the racial, ethnic, or cultural group the book represents?
- Male pronouns used to describe both males and females. Are there firefighters or firemen? Are there ancestors or forefathers?
- The book is overloaded with images of the color white as the ultimate standard of beauty, cleanliness, kindness, etc., and black as evil, bad, dirty, or unworthy.
- The heroes of color are only those that do not pose a "threat" to White establishment or authority.

This brief checklist can be beneficial in helping teachers select the right books for their diverse students without causing further harm in unintentional ways. Teachers who are effectively able to do this provide huge benefits for their students. Multicultural literature helps to establish a broader perspective and learn about similarities and differences among various cultures and groups of people. It also decreases negative stereotyping and develops positive understandings of other people and cultures. Finally, it fosters academic success by providing meaningful content to students and incorporates culturally relevant reading which engages students in the concepts being taught on a more meaningful and personal level (Cartledge et al., 2016; Iwai, 2015).

These essential elements and more are what helped my student Ryan begin to become comfortable with his new reading skills and motivated to read more! By taking the knowledge I had of his likes, interests, and family traditions, I was able to find and create leveled reading texts for him to practice and gain confidence in his skills. In starting his reading journey with mirrors, he was eventually comfortable enough to begin reading those window books he previously disliked and had no interest in. All he needed was a little familiar ground to engage in a task he was unfamiliar with: reading on his own. At the same time, providing students with culturally relevant texts shouldn't stop at our classroom door. We should also advocate for all students in the building to have access to the books they need and want. We should be creating policies and practices that allow for the accumulation and distribution of diverse texts and the training of educators to analyze books for bias while seeking the input from students, families, and community members about which books should be housed on our school library shelves (Buchanan & Fox, 2019). It takes a village!

Being committed to providing our students "windows and mirrors" experiences in the literature we select for them is an essential practice in creating school environments where all students feel welcomed and included. As educators, we must create learning experiences that validate the lives of our students and open up their minds and hearts to learning about the differences of others. In the words of Emily Style (1996):

The delightful truth is that sometimes when we hear another out, glancing through the window of their humanity, we can see our own image reflected in the glass of their window. The window becomes a mirror! And it is the shared humanity of our conversation that most impresses us even as we attend to our different frames of reference. (pp. 1-2)

Including Multiple Perspectives

"Education is the most powerful weapon which you can use to change the world" (Ratcliffe, 2017). These prophetic words uttered over three decades ago by former South African President and anti-apartheid revolutionary Nelson Rolihlahla Mandela, are still as true today as they were when he first uttered them. As most look to change the world through the accumulation of weapons and access to material goods, Mandela's suggestion that the most powerful weapon ultimately lies within our access to knowledge should not be missed by educators at large. As the gatekeepers of access to such knowledge, educators should be continually reflecting and asking themselves: Is what I teach my students going to free them to think critically enough to make positive changes in the world or perpetuate their likelihood of upholding and reproducing the repressive and dominating structures currently in place?

Brazilian activist and educator Paulo Freire also encouraged educators to empower themselves and their students towards a more emancipatory education in his classic *Pedagogy of the Oppressed* (2000). His ideas of using education as an act of freedom for oppressed and marginalized groups contradict the traditional uses of simply transferring knowledge to a liberating approach which says education should function as "...the practice of freedom, the means by which men and women deal critically and creatively with reality and discover how to participate in the transformation of their world" (Freire, 2000, p. 34). Both of these approaches were not only revolutionary in their time, but they continue to be revolutionary even today as many schools have yet to transition to this kind of teaching and learning. Any look at current statistics of the success of our educational system reveals a lack thereof for the most marginalized groups (NCES, 2017b). The stark reality of the ineffectiveness of our current methods to impart knowledge leave too many of our Black, Latinx/Hispanic, Native American, differently abled, linguistically and socioeconomically diverse students in schools without freedom-based and emancipatory learning opportunities. In order to see students' opportunities increase, this must change. Critical to this process is breaking the cycle of the single-story line and incorporating multiple perspectives in all we teach.

The unprecedented crisis of 2020 brought about challenging dilemmas in the lives of everyday Americans. A once critical society regarding the issues, concerns, and voices of those connected to the likes of the Black Lives Matter movement, many now champion and protest along with them. In what seems to be an alternate universe, one might ask: What sparked this sudden awareness and solidarity in regards to the condemnation of police brutality in the Black community? Was it in response to the brutal and recorded death of George Floyd (Hill et al., 2020)? Was it the back-to-back weaponizing of the police against Black bodies in the case of Amy Cooper (Vera & Ly, 2020); or the mother who falsely accused the drowning death of her autistic son on Black men (Miami Herald Editorial Board, 2020)? Perhaps, it was the extrajudicial killings and lynching of Breonna Taylor and Ahmad Arbury which we could not escape in our COVID-19 quarantined situations (Burke, 2020; McLaughlin, 2020)?

No matter what sparked this nation-wide outcry, these incidents, though egregious and brutal, are nothing new. Our American history has a more than 500-year legacy of violence against Black, Indigenous and other Persons of Color (BIPOC) and their communities which include but are certainly not limited to the massacres in Tulsa, Rosewood, St. Louis, and other cities (Lee & Sidner, 2020). What changed people's minds and hearts long enough to finally see today's atrocities for what they are? How did educators who were once unaware of or unbothered by the inequities their students faced become anti-racist t-shirt wearing, social media social justice warriors overnight? My theory is that for once in our hurried and over-scheduled lives we were unable to turn away from the voices and pain of others as COVID-19 has placed many of our societal ills front and center.

As educators, let's take this unprecedented moment in time to create better opportunities to help our students learn about diverse perspectives and experiences so that we can stop repeating the history of racial violence and denial for future generations. To do this, we must be ready to interrupt the "single story" narratives of our past, challenge the exclusion of marginalized voices in the knowledge construction process, and begin utilizing resources that elevate the voices of the unheard and normalize the inclusion of multiple perspectives in all we teach and do.

One-Story-Fits-All

During workshops with educators, I often use the image of an elephant to discuss the importance of multiple perspectives. In this image, five people are standing at different places around the elephant. While in their perspective places, they are all trying to describe what they see to the other participants. During this activity, the only thing anyone can see is what's in front of them. The person who can only see the tusks says "It's a spear!" The person who can only see the ears says "It's a fan!" The person who can only see the trunk says "It's a snake!" Likewise, the person who can only see the body, the tail, and leg declare those parts a rope, a tree, and a wall. Unfortunately, no one thinks to step back and put all those perspectives together to see the big picture—the elephant. No one realizes they are actually looking at an elephant because they can only see their individual viewpoints. This is typical of many instances when trying to discuss historical events and societal issues in American discourse around racism and discrimination. The "single story" of American exceptionalism, patriotism, liberty, justice for all, and meritocracy often overrides the atrocities and realities of American life that contradict those grand narratives.

Novelist Chimamanda Ngozi Adichie warns us of the dangers in a "single story" in her 2009 TED Talk when she states, "The single story creates stereotypes, and the problem with stereotypes is not that they are untrue, but that they are incomplete. They make one story become the only story" (Adichie, 2009, para. 24). Think about many of the "single story" narratives we often regard as the objective truth in our schools. Reflect on the narrative of Columbus as making the great "discovery" of America. Recall the nickname of Abraham Lincoln as "The Great Emancipator." What comes to mind if someone were to describe a Native American, African American, Asian American, Latinx/Hispanic American, White American, or a Muslim American? Are our own understandings of these events and people clouded by a single story? If so, where did these stories come from, and how did they come to dominate our thinking? For a clue, we must look at how knowledge is constructed around us, who tells us what knowledge is, and why it even matters.

Knowledge Construction Process

The knowledge construction process "describes the procedures by which social, behavioral, and natural scientists create knowledge and how the implicit cultural assumptions, frames of reference, perspectives, and biases within a discipline influence the ways that knowledge is constructed within it" (Banks, 2019, p. 45). This process encourages higher levels of education by helping students understand concepts and events from multiple perspectives. A true conscious educator understands that when knowledge is only presented from one viewpoint, one cannot get the full understanding of its meaning. Because all knowledge is tainted by the cultural lenses of the knower, we must have more than one understanding of the world in order to understand its complexity. This will ultimately allow us to help our students think more consciously and critically about the world. Unfortunately, in America, many of our deeply held beliefs about our history, practices, and views of diverse people stem from the perspective of the wealthy, White, male. When educators understand how the knowledge construction process works, they can help challenge the dominance of the perspectives of the White and middle-class and make room for the funds of knowledge and the community cultural wealth of marginalized groups (Moll et al., 1992; Yosso, 2005).

The funds of knowledge approach (Gonzales et al., 2005; Yamauchi et al., 2017), and community cultural wealth (Yosso, 2005) are approaches that challenge the superiority of dominant norms and frame the cultural knowledge and experiences of marginalized groups as worthy of value and inclusion (Parker & Lynn, 2002). These two approaches remove the hierarchy of knowledge put in place across many sectors in American life and place them on the same level as those perspectives held by the dominant class. This process is upsetting for many and resistance is inevitable. Whether we realize it or not, this process is already taking place all across America. The debate over and the act of taking down Confederate monuments has many experiencing the cognitive dissonance of multiple perspectives (Aguilera, 2020). While some argue the removal of these statues removes "our" history, others note that the hoisting of memorials for enemies of the country is hardly to be praised (Wise, 2017).

Nonetheless, the knowledge construction process necessary for a multiple perspectives approach will help us create a more critical understanding of the world for ourselves and our students. Those single stories of Columbus "discovering America" can be countered with the voices of the Arawak and Taino people he and his men enslaved, maimed, and slaughtered during their "discovery" (Zinn, 2003). Claims that Abraham Lincoln was the sole and benevolent "Great Emancipator" can be countered with the transcripts from his correspondence between Frederick Douglass, other abolitionists, and speeches in which he stated that his only mission was to "save the Union" and that he did not believe Blacks were equal to Whites (Foner, 2000). A multiple perspectives approach will turn the negative racial stereotypes pushed onto us from birth about the laziness, savagery, and inferiority of BIPOC in literature, television, music, and movies, to be countered with historical analysis of the treatment of marginalized groups at the hands of the majority White U.S. government and citizenry alike (Takaki, 2008; Zinn, 2003). Many of us are trapped, as James Baldwin said it "in a history they don't understand" (1962). As mostly

White citizens attempted a coup in the U.S. Capitol at the beginning of 2021, claims that "this is not who we are," or that these events are somehow an anomaly, dismiss the very real and very similar manner past White racial uprisings happened in America. We can release ourselves from this trap of historical inaccuracy and hegemonic, monocultural single stories by committing to a multiple perspective approach in all we do.

Including Multiple Perspectives

To do this, we must invest in the utilization of resources that incorporate the cultures, histories, perspectives, and experiences of marginalized groups and people. We must be able to identify where these gaps exist in our curriculum and incorporate materials and learning opportunities that provide practice in understanding diverse perspectives. We must support our students in the practice of asking questions, acknowledging opinions, and being open-minded in discussions where multiple views exist. Only then can we see the "elephant" in the room in many of our classroom and school settings which support the dominance of White cultural norms and narratives in our teaching and replace it with more inclusive and multiple perspective approaches.

To begin, we must have a storehouse of supplemental resources to help. Teachers can add these books to their learning library: *Lies My Teacher Told Me: Everything Your American History Textbook Got Wrong* (Loewen, 2007); *Sundown Towns: A Hidden Dimension of American Racism* (Loewen, 2005); *Stamped from the Beginning: The Definitive History of Racist Ideas in America* (Kendi, 2016); *A Different Mirror: A History of Multicultural America* (Takaki, 2008); and *An African American and Latinx History of the United States* (Ortiz, 2018). This list is by no means exhaustive but can get teachers on the right track. There are even student versions of many of these books such as *A Young People's History of the United States: Columbus to the War on Terror (For Young People Series)* (Zinn & Stefoff, 2009); *Stamped: Racism, Antiracism, and You: A Remix of the National Book Award-winning Stamped from the Beginning* (Reynolds & Kendi, 2020); and *Encounter* (Yolen & Shannon, 1996) among many,

many others! Below is a list of resources that we can use to supplement our curriculum and practices with multiple perspectives so that all students can not only see themselves and others, but *hear* themselves and others too.

Supplemental Resources for Multiple Perspectives

Zinn Education Project
www.zinned.org

Teaching for Change
www.teachingforchange.org

Social Justice Books
www.socialjusticebooks.org

Lee and Low Books
www.leeandlow.com

The Trevor Project
https://www.thetrevorproject.org/resources/

Good Docs
https://gooddocs.net/

The Brown Bookshelf
https://thebrownbookshelf.com/

Black Lives Matter at School Week
https://blacklivesmatteratschool.com/

We Need Diverse Books
https://diversebooks.org/resources/where-to-find-diverse-books/

Hijab Librarians
https://hijabilibrarians.com/

Latinos' in Kid Lit
https://latinosinkidlit.com/

Indigo's Bookshelf
https://indigosbookshelf.blogspot.com/

American Indians in Children's Literature
https://americanindiansinchildrensliterature.blogspot.com/?m=1

Disability in Kid Lit
http://disabilityinkidlit.com/honor-roll/

Ultimately, by allowing more opportunities for students to think critically about the information they receive, we give students the freedom to become investigators of knowledge, not just regurgitators of facts and dates. When we make the inclusion of multiple perspectives common practice in our teaching methods, we free students from the false narratives of single stories that seek to reduce our humanity and null and void our worthiness. In other words, "It is only by disrupting single stories with narratives told from other perspectives that we form a more nuanced picture of the people, issues, or ideas at hand" (Tschida et al., 2014, p. 31). Let the disruption continue.

Creating Inclusive School Policies

If you met me during my middle/high school years, you probably would not have pegged me to one day become an educator, an author, a small business owner, a college graduate, or a Ph.D. student. Let's just say that my middle/high school experiences led most to see me as most likely *not* to succeed and more likely to be in trouble. Like most adolescents, I struggled with the growing pains of developing social and emotional maturity. Developing friendships, navigating romantic relationships, and trying to figure out who I was and where I "fit" within my social, academic, and athletic environments were often turbulent. As a young Black female in these situations, these already common adolescent milestones were compounded by colorism within my own racial/ethnic community. It was sprinkled with micro and macro aggressions from non-Black friends and teachers; while racism, discrimination, and implicit/explicit bias from non-Black students, teachers, and coaches was never far behind. Unfortunately, the low-expectations, selective perceptions, and tone (and facial) policing imposed on me beginning in my adolescent years were not simply unique to me alone. Educational research will echo my experiences as common for many young Black girls. Research explains that Black girls are not only more likely to experience adultification and criminalization for normal adolescent behaviors, but overall are seen as less innocent, older, more sexually advanced, angry (even when not), and less in need of protection than our White counterparts (Anderson, 2016; Halberstadt & Shipman, 2020; Ruiz-Grossman, 2019).

Monique W. Morris' documentary film *Pushout: The Criminalization of Black Girls in Schools* (Atlas, 2019) illustrates on screen the harsh reality of the practices, policies, and beliefs that affect the social, emotional, and academic lives of young Black girls. This film, which is based off of her 2016 book by the same name, puts into perspective a glaring and questionable disparity in our school discipline policies. If Black girls are only 16 percent of the student population, why are they also 48 percent of the population that is expelled and nearly one-third of all referrals to law enforcement and actual arrests in schools (Morris, 2016)? The answers lie less in the question of "What are these girls doing to get into trouble?" and more in "What is it about our school culture, beliefs, practices, and policies that continue to criminalize these girls for common adolescent behaviors their White counterparts are allowed to learn and grow from?"

For the answer, we look to the evidence which says the zero-tolerance policies in many public schools are hurting students more than helping (Hoffman, 2014; Milner et al., 2019). In particular, current school discipline policies disproportionately harm Black students in general as they are being punished three times more than their White counterparts for the same offenses (Hoffman, 2014; Lamboy et al., 2020; Williams et al., 2018). Many of these discipline disparities are contributing to social phenomena such as the school-to-prison pipeline and high rates of dropouts among many Black students (American Civil Liberties Union, 2020). Are Black kids simply just "bad students"? Are they "dropping out" because they are unmotivated to succeed? The better question is: Are we *pushing* them out? How we frame this issue ultimately determines our response to it. If *they* are the problem (students and families), then there's nothing we can do. But if *we* are the problem (school practices and policies), then we must change how we approach the students and families we serve and make the necessary changes in our disciplinary practices and policies to serve them better. To do this, we will need a new lens to see the issues we face and updated skills and knowledge to bring such changes to fruition. To begin creating inclusive schools where all students feel safe and can stay connected to their learning environments begins with understanding two things: (a) How well current school practices are working to create safe and inclusive environments for all students; (b) Effective alternative practices that repair harm and allow students to learn and grow from mistakes. We need to take a closer look at our obsession with control and punishment in discipline and move towards the promises of restorative practices.

Zero Tolerance Produces Zero Benefits

What is the most common method schools use to address unwanted or offensive behaviors in humans? If your answer was contextual analysis in understanding the root causes of such behaviors and opportunities to understand how those behaviors affect the perpetrator and the victim, you'd be wrong. If you said exclusionary, control-based, and punitive measures which remove unwanted individuals and separate the "good" from the "bad," you'd be right on the money. For centuries, the dominant method in Western society has taken a "crime and punishment" attitude towards all forms of misbehavior in society and schools. Many Americans agree with this and believe a "law and order" approach is the best way to maintain a peaceful society. The evidence of our "success" in this area rests in the fact that the U.S. is not only not the most peaceful country in the world, we also lead the world in incarceration rates at 22 percent. To put this number in perspective, we are less than 5 percent of the world's population (Ye Hee Lee, 2015).

In schools, similar punitive approaches reveal themselves as "Zero-Tolerance" policies which are defined as "a school or district policy that mandates predetermined consequence/s or punishment for specific offenses" (U.S. Department of Education, 1998, p. 18). These policies were initially enacted to reduce the occurrence of students bringing lethal weapons or illegal drugs to school but have evolved into covering less egregious offenses such as dress code violations as well (Hoffman, 2014). Researchers revealed that zero-tolerance policies which were intended to create safe and compliant schools actually ended up exacerbating suspension rates and drop-out rates, worsened school climates, and lowered student achievement (Raffaele Mendez & Knoff, 2003; Skiba & Rausch, 2006). Not only that, but zero-tolerance policies are also responsible for exacerbating the current racial disparities in discipline rates where Black and Latinx students are often the recipients of these forms of punishments for infractions such as dress code violations, swearing, and truancy (American Psychological Association Zero Tolerance Task Force, 2008; Milner et al., 2019). If the evidence is clear that these kinds of policies do nothing to keep students safe and, in fact, disproportionately punish and push kids out of schools and into prisons, why do we still utilize these practices? Taking a cue from Kenya Barris' latest and controversial show *#BlackAF* (Netflix, 2020), this too, is because of slavery.

Public School Education as Slavery by Another Name

The year 1619 marks the date some historians use to describe when the European enslavement of Africans officially kicked off in the U.S. (Kendi, 2016; Zinn, 2003). Critics of this date will remind us that slavery existed long before in the U.S. as Spanish explorer Lucas Vasquez de

Ayllon brought 500 Europeans and 100 enslaved Africans from Haiti in 1526 (Meltzer, 1971). However, for contextual purposes of the discussion ahead, we will begin in 1619 (Serwer, 2019). In 1619 some "twenty and odd Negroes" were brought off of a Dutch man-of-war ship to what would later become Virginia (Brown, 2018). The European colonizers, like Ayllon, who sought to stake their claim to the "New World " also brought indentured servants from home. Although the European indentured servants were not treated much better than the enslaved Africans were, many of the colonial laws during the seventeenth century were instrumental in ushering in the distinction that would eventually lead to the "problem of the color-line" (Du Bois, 1994; Meltzer, 1971; Zinn, 2003).

This "color-line" would be the catalyst for race relations in America for centuries to come. These laws were attempts to discourage disenfranchised Black and White people from joining forces in insurrection against the White wealthy elites which exploited them both (Zinn, 2003). The racist justifications that would emerge out of these laws which criminalized blackness in every imaginable way made it easier for the institutions of American slavery, Jim Crow, segregation, and mass incarceration to inflict psychological and physical trauma on Black men, women, and children from its onset until today (Alexander, 2012; Kendi, 2016). These justifications have been embedded in the psyche of all Americans and have fueled many of the racial stereotypes about Black inferiority still in use today. Similarly, the act of restricting enslaved Africans' access to knowledge through outlawing reading, writing, and formal schooling (Douglass, 1968) and later by providing inferior educational opportunities reinforced the ideas of Black inferiority as "knowledge."

Carter G. Woodson coined this process of false education as *miseducation* when he described the purpose of schooling back in 1933 by stating:

> As another has well said, to handicap a student by teaching him that his black face is a curse and that his struggle to change his condition is hopeless is the worst sort of lynching. It kills one's

aspirations and dooms him to vagabondage and crime. It is strange, then, that the friends of truth and the promoters of freedom have not risen up against the present propaganda in the schools and crushed it. This crusade is much more important than the anti-lynching movement, because there would be no lynching if it did not start in the schoolroom. Why not exploit, enslave, or exterminate a class that everybody is taught to regard as inferior! (p. 3)

The anti-blackness of the past has not disappeared as some would like to think. The roots of much of the anti-black sentiments of the past are alive and well today. Many of these manifestations carry on in society and are reinforced every year in our classrooms and schools.

My comparisons of the modern-day school system to the institution of slavery may seem dramatic or far-fetched to some. However, if you've made it this far in the book and have paid any attention to the continued and current racialized ills our students continue to face in our schools, it would almost be an act of willful ignorance to not see the patterns and connections. Regardless of the legislative milestones (e.g., *Brown vs. Board*) or individual successes (Lebron James, Barack Obama, Oprah Winfrey, etc.) marginalized groups have made in spite of this system, it must be understood that even though *some* were able to "make it," they did so against the intended purposes of education as subjugation and the reinforcement of White supremacy in America. Why must future generations continue to face those hurdles?

When we honestly and critically reflect on our current school practices and policies, we will inevitably see the connections between American slavery and the American school system (Ball, 2006; Gatto, 2017; Johnson, 2019). As Gatto (2017) poignantly states: "Schools teach exactly what they are intended to teach…: how to be a good Egyptian and remain in your place in the pyramid" (p. 13). From pre-kindergarten to senior year, American schools are set up to track, over-discipline, under and mis-educate, suspend, expel, dehumanize, and indoctrinate to the cultural norms, values, behaviors, and beliefs of a White, male, English-speaking, middle to upper class way of being (Johnson, 2019).

American schools are notorious for disproportionally providing Black students with lower-level classwork (Gay, 2010). Nationwide statistics on school discipline disparities continue to show the over-disciplining of Black, Latinx, and Native American students compared to their White counterparts (Milner et al., 2019). The curriculum bolstered as "high-quality" learning is dominated by White, middle-class knowledge which combines the distortion, erasure, and exclusion of marginalized perspectives, experiences, histories, and contributions (King, 2020; Ladson-Billings, 1995). All of which is reinforced by its White and female dominated education force (the unwitting slave masters) to ensure this kind of subjugation, manipulation, and miseducation is rendered "impolite," "inappropriate," and "disrespectful" to rebel against as the dissent of teachers of color are policed and silenced into submission just as much as the students are (Morrison, 2019).

In short, the schools that we claim are the 'great equalizers' and pathways toward freedom have been nothing more than modern day Indian boarding schools (Adams, 1995) which reinforce unquestioned White authority through its curriculum, policies, practices and teaching force. Today's recent and sudden protests from teachers against racism will mean nothing in upcoming school years if the roots of the racial inequities in our society are not first addressed and eradicated in our racist schools.

Better Teachers, Better Schools, Better Society, Better World

The overturning of the long-held grip that racism has had on the American school system will come at a price that many may not want to pay. In order to usher in a new era in the purpose and function of schooling and move towards truly equitable, inclusive, and emancipatory approaches, we must be willing to let go of the comforts that our former White dominated school practices brought us and be open to including more diverse, multicultural, culturally responsive, and restorative approaches. Ultimately, we must be willing to reinvest in the effectiveness of those who are in charge of creating such environments.

The truth of the matter is, if we truly want to create better schools, we've got to prepare teachers in a better way.

Effective teachers will be the catalyst that holds all that is discussed throughout the pages of this book together. Teachers' willingness to let go of methods that they thought were "good teaching" and replace them with methods that are more aligned with our "all students can learn" values should be followed up with approaches that actually provide equitable opportunities for that learning to take place. The promises of culturally relevant pedagogy (Ladson-Billings, 2009) and culturally responsive teaching (Gay, 2010) have decades of educational research behind them, which informs our need to have teachers who can embody these approaches. Culturally responsive/relevant pedagogies ensure that educators no longer see students as 'blank slates' but know they all possess individual and cultural knowledge and strengths and that those aspects should be utilized to create classroom environments which *embrace* them and their diversity, *empower* them to develop agency, *educate* them in their histories, and *include* their voices and experiences in shaping school policies and practices (Banks, 2019; Gay, 2010; Ladson-Billings, 2009).

Educational scholars Valerie Hill-Jackson and Delia Stafford's 2017 book *Better Teachers, Better Schools: What Star Teachers Know, Believe, and Do* highlights that in order for us to have schools equipped with teachers who can create the positive and successful learning environments for diverse students, we must be willing to reassess not only what we thought was good teaching, but who we believe a good teacher to be. This reflective work begins by understanding "too many teachers who are designated to urban or diverse classrooms do not have the mindset to be an effective teacher" (Hill-Jackson & Stafford, 2017, p. xv). These approaches are more than strategies, resources, and printables. In order for educators to be effective for diverse students, they must think like culturally responsive educators before they can act on it. Effective culturally responsive educators know and understand their diverse students and the most equitable ways to teach them. Equipping every educator with the knowledge and skills needed to become a conscious educator is the ultimate goal! It will be hard work and not all teachers will be able to embody these practices. However, the work must continue. All students deserve to have their education delivered by educators who are not only interested in maintaining their culture and humanity, but restoring it when it is at risk of being erased. This can be done not only through responsive teaching but restorative practices as well.

Restorative practices will be needed to overturn many of the negative statistics regarding racial disparities in discipline in our schools (Advancement Project, 2014; Taylor, 2020). If we truly want to create schools that are safe and responsive, we must take heed of the recommendations in restorative discipline practices. *The Institute for Restorative Justice and Restorative Dialogue* (https://irjrd.org/) is a great resource for teachers looking for a more in-depth understanding of these approaches. Also, please check out the resources available through *The International Institute for Restorative Practices* (bit.ly/2Vasw4H) and *The Schott Foundation* (schottfoundation.org/restorativejustice). The following discussion, which will close out this chapter, will provide a short overview of this approach and how it can help us bring to fruition those wholly inclusive school atmospheres we value for all students.

Restoring Our Schools Through Restorative Practices

As a whole, restorative discipline's intent revolves around "a mindset, and an approach to discipline that builds upon the foundational idea that schools are places where students are expected to make errors and learn from them" (Milner et al., 2019, p. 133). It involves the understanding that, "instead of removing and excluding students from their educational setting as punishment, a restorative discipline approach supports students coming to terms with how their actions may have affected others, taking responsibility for these actions, and continuing to learn and grow" (Milner et al., 2019, p. 133). Key to the successful implementation of these processes is the belief in fairness, equity, and justice in school discipline practices. Our goals should be to move away from the practice of punishment in addressing student behaviors and move towards creating classrooms and schools in which no student is excluded from the environment. We should be determined to create spaces where all students have the chance to learn and grow from their mistakes. These beliefs combined with the goals of building relationships, reducing and preventing harmful behavior, resolving conflict, repairing harm, and addressing needs of the school community (Advancement Project, 2014) are essential understandings for educators to ensure these approaches work. Implementing restorative approaches in schools in an effort to reduce and eliminate the racial disparities in discipline rates and create safe and inclusive schools for all relies on the use of three necessary methods: affective language, circle processes, and restorative conferences.

Affective Language, Circle Processes, and Restorative Conferences

The largest component of implementing restorative discipline rests in the practice of using affective language. Affective language consists of statements and questioning that "genuinely expresses feelings or emotions related to specific behaviors or actions of others (Milner et al., 2019, p. 139). Affective language provides a structure for reinforcing desired behaviors and redirecting unwanted ones" (Costello et al., 2009). The purpose of utilizing these kinds of statements is to help students understand how their actions have affected others (George, 2017). According to Costello et al. (2009), when utilizing these statements educators should:

- Focus on specific behaviors while not confusing this with the worth of the student.
- Provide students an opportunity to observe the consequences of their behavior.
- Consider if a private conversation is better than a public one.
- Ensure more positive statements are used for every corrective statement.

According to Costello et al. (2009) and findings from the San Francisco Unified School District (2010), teachers and schools can use the following examples of affective statements and questions offered by experts:

Statements:

- I appreciate you/your…
- I feel frustrated when I see/hear/…
- It excites me to see/hear…
- I am angry about…
- It makes me uncomfortable to hear/see…

Questions:

- What happened?
- What were you thinking when this happened?
- What have you thought about since?
- Who has been affected by what you did?
- How have they been affected?
- What do you think you can do to make this right?

Circle processes are the next step in the restorative process as these circles are used to build and restore relationships to create and sustain a sense of community (Milner et al., 2019). It is suggested by Zher (2015) that these circles be used proactively as part of the classroom routine and reactively to solve problems when they arise. The use of these restorative circles provides a safe way for victims and offenders to address concerns and allows for student ownership of the conflict resolution process, interrupts the school-to-prison pipeline as students are allowed to stay in class to resolve issues not sent to detention, suspension, etc., and ultimately provides a remedy to the harm done (Ortega et al., 2016).

Milner et al. (2019) suggests to making restorative circles part of your daily classroom or school practices by:

- Creating daily time for students to sit in a circle in the form of a morning meeting or community circle, etc.
- Allowing students to facilitate or co-facilitate the sessions by allowing them to discuss issues that affect them.
- Allowing students to reflect at the end of the day, share personal stories, or resolve minor issues among students.

The final step in implementing restorative discipline practices rests in conducting restorative conferences to repair serious harms or address personal crises for students. These conferences are usually used to resolve conflicts, discuss what happened, and work together to find a solution to make it right in a more intimate setting (Amstutz & Mullet, 2005). These conferences differ from restorative circles as they do not address community needs but they do address specific conflicts between individuals. Successful implementation of these smaller and individualized conferences is likely if a few key components are kept in mind.

First, ensure that these conferences are facilitated by those who can be viewed as impartial (Shaw & Wierenga, 2002). Next, ensure these conferences only include those directly involved so that solutions are specific enough to address the situational needs of all those involved. Finally, questions during these conferences should be open-ended enough to prompt all involved to find solutions to repair harm to the broken relationships.

Please utilize the following question stems to help (Davidson, 2014; Milner, 2019):

- Tell me what's been happening?
- What has not been working well for you?
- How are you feeling about this situation?
- How is this getting in the way of your learning?

- Do you feel like you can be the person you want to be at school?
- How can you make things right? What can I/we do to support you?
- What do you think you would do differently if this situation occurs again?

Overall, the previous breakdown of the restorative discipline process for classrooms and schools can help create the positive, caring, safe, and inclusive learning environments both teachers and students deserve. However, reversing the trends in racial disparities in our school discipline practices and policies will not happen overnight and will not happen without a shared commitment from educators, school leaders, students, families, and the community at large. It will take a village to help all students feel safe. It will take a village *mindset* to break the chains that individualism and competition have had on us for far too long. Combining the promises of culturally responsive/relevant pedagogies and restorative practices will get us closer to the mountaintop of positive, inclusive, and culturally responsive and equitable schools for all.

SEL for ALL

A final but foundational and necessary component in creating inclusive school environments is dependent on the presence and effective practice and implementation of social-emotional learning in schools. According to the Collaborative for Academic, Social, and Emotional Learning (2020) (CASEL), social and emotional learning (SEL) is "the process through which children and adults understand and manage emotions, set and achieve positive goals, feel and show empathy for others, establish and maintain positive relationships, and make responsible decisions." CASEL defines this process through five competencies of self-awareness, self-management, social awareness, relationship skills, and responsible decision-making (CASEL, 2020). Needless to say,

SEL is the glue that holds inclusive school practices together as when they are at the foundation, they inherently help us create and maintain more positive, equitable, safe, and authentically inclusive environments. However, SEL has become one of the latest buzzwords in school reform and many have jumped on the SEL bandwagon without much critical reflection on how it can be applied in our multi-racial classrooms and schools.

Infusing SEL competencies with culturally responsive practices is key in creating positive school environments, promoting high expectations, and fostering caring learning environments which aid in academic achievement of all students (Donahue-Keegan et al., 2019). Teachers with a solid background in social-emotional learning and cultural competency are better equipped to support the academic achievement of marginalized communities than those who do not hold such capacities. Culturally responsive teachers know how to approach students through a strengths-based lens; those without this mindset often use SEL practices to simply "fix" or "control" the behavior of seemingly noncompliant diverse students (Hoffman, 2009). SEL without context of the larger sociopolitical context that marginalized students experience and void of the consideration of inequitable structures in place is just "White supremacy with a hug" (Madda, 2019). According to Dena Simmons (as cited in Madda, 2019), SEL does more harm than good if we avoid discussing the issues that are creating the unsettling emotional reactions students are exhibiting when dealing with racial stressors and provides educators with a few important strategies for implementing what she calls "fearless" SEL.

Strategies for Fearless SEL

According to Simmons (2019), when implementing equitable opportunities for "fearless" SEL, teachers should:

- Provide students with opportunities to reflect on identity and how their identity can pose barriers or opportunities in the world (self-awareness).

- Provide students opportunities to participate in debates and work cross-culturally with those who are different from themselves (building relationships).
- Utilize community-based projects to help students work together to solve issues that are important to them in their communities (decision-making skills).
- Create opportunities for students to study current events and social movements (social awareness).
- Provide students with an understanding of the different expectations that are placed on different identity groups when regulating their emotions (self-management). For example, men are viewed as strong when they do not emit emotions, while women are seen as hysterical, weak, or irrational when they do. The same can be observed across racial differences as Black people are expected to regulate their emotions more strictly when faced with racist or discriminatory actions than other racial groups (Simmons, 2019).

These practices, intended to help students, must also be modeled by teachers. A culturally responsive SEL approach cannot be established without these competencies and dispositions being embedded with the everyday mindset and practices of the educators which utilize them. Teachers must understand that in developing social and emotional skills, they have to also come with a culturally responsive background. We can't have one without the other. Frequent opportunities for educators to engage in critical self-reflection and developing their own social-emotional stamina is key in this practice.

Essentially, SEL cannot happen in decontextualized environments. SEL must be connected to the lived experiences of the students it is intended to serve. If SEL efforts are only utilized to control or make compliant students and manage their behaviors without addressing the environmental inequities that also affect them, we are not doing social-emotional work. We are doing social-emotional harm by ignoring unjust systems. Teaching students to regulate their emotions, make responsible decisions, or build positive relationships while ignoring or being ignorant of the racist and unjust systems and individuals that trigger anti-social behaviors misses the opportunity to empower students to dismantle those systems. Instead, they are being asked to cope more "pleasantly," without upsetting the dominant (White) cultural norms and the inequitable environments that they are subjected to.

Creating inclusive school environments is a goal many schools aim for, but many are struggling to create. Decades-long inequity and repressive practices in schools still continue to grip the reins in shaping many school cultures and climates. Only through intentional and concentrated commitments to improve the school environment will the promises of culturally responsive, equitable, restorative, socially and emotionally safe schools no longer be a goal but a reality.

Questions for Reflection

1. Are there disparities in the discipline rates in your classroom or school? If so, how have you or do you plan to address them to create more equitable outcomes?
2. Reflect on a recent interaction with a student regarding misbehavior. How did you address it? Was further harm caused by implementing a punitive punishment? Was the student removed from the school setting? Do you think a restorative approach would have helped in this situation?
3. How have you worked to develop your knowledge and skills in becoming a culturally conscious educator? Have you had opportunities to develop a mindset committed to justice and equity? If not, how do you plan to move towards this in the future?
4. How can you begin to advocate for restorative discipline programs for your schools? What barriers to this endeavor do you anticipate?

5. What level of social and emotional learning is evident in your classroom or school practices? How do you address the sociopolitical factors that affect students' ability to demonstrate the characteristics of social and emotional competence?

6. ALL MEANS ALL

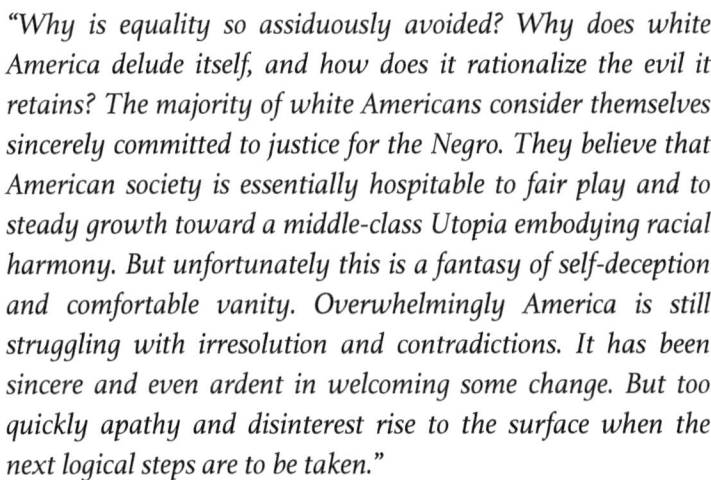
"Why is equality so assiduously avoided? Why does white America delude itself, and how does it rationalize the evil it retains? The majority of white Americans consider themselves sincerely committed to justice for the Negro. They believe that American society is essentially hospitable to fair play and to steady growth toward a middle-class Utopia embodying racial harmony. But unfortunately this is a fantasy of self-deception and comfortable vanity. Overwhelmingly America is still struggling with irresolution and contradictions. It has been sincere and even ardent in welcoming some change. But too quickly apathy and disinterest rise to the surface when the next logical steps are to be taken."

— Dr. Martin Luther King, Jr., *Where Do We Go from Here? Community or Chaos*, 1968, pp. 4-5

Let's go back to the beginning for a moment and think again about the following statement: The continued presence of the racial achievement gap is not merely an indication of how poorly individual students perform, but more of an indication of a school's lack of effectiveness to teach certain students. Is this statement true or false? After reading through the previous chapters, is your answer still the same, or has it changed? If your answer remains the same and you still believe the disparities in our schools lay solely at the feet of the students who experience them, what solutions are you willing to put forth to end those disparities? If your answer changed and you now believe schools are not doing all they can to meet the needs of all students, what are you going to do differently to make sure change happens in the future? All of this boils down to response and action. What is your response to the continued disparities in student achievement and opportunity, and what actions are you willing to take to help eradicate them? The four principles for conscious educators can reveal to us that no reform can happen until we are *collectively willing* to engage in the actions necessary to allow it to happen. If we say we want *all* students to succeed, then *all* teachers need to be equipped to make it happen. All means *all*. It's time for real change!

This school year, let's continue the process of becoming more conscious teachers and schools. Let's move past the comfortable practices that maintain the appearance of perfect institutions, maintain the status quo, and become dedicated to authentic self-reflection, institutional growth, and positive cultural change. Let's stop playing the blame game, which points the finger at students and families experiencing the racial and class disparities present within our schools, and instead open our arms to embrace them and work together in mutual accountability for *all* of our students. As teacher populations remain 80 percent White (Miller, 2018) and student populations continue to grow increasingly more diverse, those in charge of educating all students need to begin to hold all teachers accountable for any lack of knowledge or actionable response in the racial achievement and discipline disparities our students face. Yes, many teachers claim to disavow racism and discrimination online and on t-shirts; yet, many of their actions of apathy and complacency are speaking louder than their words and performative allyship.

The promising solutions outlined throughout this book will bring an end to the racism, inequity, and lack of educational opportunity in our schools. If we want our teachers to be effective in educating culturally, linguistically, socioeconomically, religiously diverse, and differently-abled students, they must be trained to recognize inequity, check their racial bias, and implement steps to reduce its impact on their students (Young, 2016). Eliminating the unchecked biases and racist assumptions many teachers hold about their diverse students is not another attempt at political correctness. The racism that students of color experience at the hands of culturally clueless educators harms their academic achievement and their potential to create a path for success in the world. Research has shown that teachers lower their expectations for students who are poor, students of color, and who have special needs (Arditi, 2014; Rubie-Davies, 2018). Teachers who hold negative views about their poor and students of color expect less of them, give them less challenging work, and often discipline them more often and more harshly than White students who act in similar ways (Long, 2016). Students exposed to this kind of treatment from educators often experience the phenomenon of self-fulfilling prophecy and often fall in line with the negative assumptions teachers project onto their abilities (Positive Psychology Program, 2018). Teachers, we can change these outcomes!

The portrayal of these issues as racist is not an overreaction; they're evidence that the racism that permeates throughout society is also present within the walls of our schools. However, it's not impossible to shield our students from the snares of societal ills. As an experienced educator and facilitator, I understand we are in an uphill battle; however, I believe a solid investment in anti-racist, culturally responsive, and equity-focused education for all teachers is the first step. Will it be easy? Absolutely not. Nevertheless, any time and effort put forth in the process are well worth the results of more culturally conscious teachers and schools in the future.

It can be troubling work to reevaluate deeply held beliefs about race and class in education. However, reexamining our deeply held views about these issues has often propelled our society towards its espoused ideas of justice and equality. It's happening right now! Let's keep the momentum going and continue to reevaluate what we thought was "not racist" to become truly culturally responsive and anti-racist educators and schools. I resolve to continue the hard work to help educators rid our schools of racist mindsets and replace them with ones that no longer have to apologize for racially insensitive missteps because the roots of their racism will have been destroyed. Again, hard work and action are key to this lasting change.

Looking back at the opening quote from Dr. Martin Luther King, Jr., it rings true as the sad reality of the complacency many educators and school leaders are stuck in when faced with the challenge of moving towards actionable change. Just replace his observations of liberal Whites during the Civil Rights Movement with the teachers of today. Just replace "White American" with the words "teachers" or "schools." Let's try it!

> "Why is equality so assiduously avoided? Why [do] schools delude [themselves], and how does it rationalize the evil it retains? The majority of [teachers] consider themselves sincerely committed to justice for [students]. They believe that American [schools are] essentially hospitable to fair play and to steady growth toward [academic achievement and] racial harmony. But unfortunately, this is a fantasy of self-deception and comfortable vanity. Overwhelmingly [schools are] still struggling with irresolution and contradictions. It has been sincere and even ardent in welcoming some change. But too quickly apathy and disinterest rise to the surface when the next logical steps are to be taken."

The next logical step is equity in schools. The path to getting there is through the four principles of equity for conscious educators, which embrace, empower, educate, and include every student, every day! To do this, a greater commitment toward action is needed from us all to take a step out of the darkness of our comfort zones towards the light of true equitable school environments. A more significant commitment is required from teacher-educators, administrators, stakeholders, policy-makers, teachers, and parents to hold not only themselves, but each other accountable for creating culturally responsive, positive, caring, and equitable school environments for every student. This accountability should not just be rooted in calling out racism and discrimination in schools but also calling in those stuck in the comforting grips of the traditions and complacency of White hegemony and guiding them in grace, mercy, knowledge, and love towards true multicultural change. Because no one should be on this journey alone, only together will we be able to brave the deep waters of educational inequality.

Together, we can move more profoundly into authentic, equitable, and culturally responsive practices. Together, we can create schools where all students feel welcomed, valued, and included. If we are ready, we can embrace the change that will take us on a journey that will help us transform our schools and ourselves. It is time for teachers to become uncomfortable with being comfortable on the surface of their diversity, equity, and inclusion efforts in schools. It is time to make deeper commitments to cultural responsiveness, anti-racism, and equity in education, not just for ourselves but for *all* of our students.

Questions for Reflection

1. How can your campus become a place where all students are seen, valued, and heard?
2. What can your school do to better embody the principles of a conscious educator?
3. Reflect on your school policies. Which ones can you eliminate to help create a more positive and culturally responsive environment?
4. How can administrators support teachers in growing their effectiveness in conscious practices?

ABOUT THE AUTHOR

Salandra Grice is a former educator and the founder of Conscious Education Consulting, LLC. Her company provides professional development in culturally responsive, equity-based, anti-bias/anti-racist, and anti-oppressive teaching practices. Her mission is to help educators create equitable and positive learning experiences for every student through dynamic, interactive, reflective, and transformative professional development for teachers and schools. Please send comments and requests for information on consulting, workshops, or speaking opportunities to conscioused18@gmail.com, or visit www.consciousednow.com.

REFERENCES

Adams, D. W. (1995). *Education for extinction: American Indians and the boarding schoo experience, 1875-1928.* Lawrence: University Press of Kansas.

Adichie, C. N. (2009, July). *The danger of a single story* [Video]. TED.

Advancement Project. (2014). *Restorative practices: Fostering healthy relationships & promoting positive discipline in schools.* The Schott Foundation for Public Education.

Aguilera, J. (2020, June 9). *Confederate statues are being removed amid protests over George Floyd's death. Here's what to know.* Time. https://time.com/5849184/confederate-statues-removed/

Alexander, M. (2010, 2012). *The new Jim Crow: Mass incarceration in the age of colorblindness.* The New Press.

American Civil Liberties Union. (2020, July 31). *School-to-prison pipeline.* American Civil Liberties Union. https://www.aclu.org/issues/juvenile-justice/school-prison-pipeline

American Psychological Association Zero Tolerance Task Force. (2008). Are zero tolerance policies effect in the schools? An evidentiary review and recommendations. *American Psychologist, 63,* 852–862. https://doi.org/10.1037/0003-066X.63.9.852

Amstutz, L. S., & Mullet, J. H. (2005). *The little book of restorative discipline for schools: Teaching responsibility; creating caring climates.* Good Books.

Anderson, M. D. (2016, March 8a). *The academic benefits of ethnic studies.* The Atlantic. https://www.theatlantic.com/education/archive/2016/03/the-ongoing-battle-over-ethnic-studies/472422/

Anderson, M. D. (2016, March 15b). *The criminalization of Black girls in schools.* The Atlantic. https://www.theatlantic.com/education/archive/2016/03/the-criminalization-of-black-girls-in-schools/473718/

Anderson, J. D. (1988). *The education of Blacks in the south, 1860-1935.* University of Nort Carolina Press.

Arditi, T. (2014, October 6). Teachers have lower expectations for students of color and students from low-income backgrounds. *Center for American Progress.* https://www.americanprogress.org/press/release/2014/10/06/98317/release-teachers-have-lower-expectations-for-students-of-color-and-students-from-low-income-backgrounds/

Aschoff, N. (2020, March 21). *Coronavirus has exposed America's digital divide*. Jacobin. https://www.jacobinmag.com/2020/03/coronavirus-digital-classrooms-cambridge-schools-internet-broadband-access

Atlas, J. (Director) (2019). *Pushout: The criminalization of Black girls in schools* [film]. Monique W. Morris. https://pushoutfilm.com/film

Auerbach, S. (2010). Beyond coffee with the principal: Toward leadership for authentic school-family partnerships. *Journal of School Leadership, 20*(6), 728–757.

Baker, T. L., Wise, J., Kelley, G., & Skiba, R. J. (2016). Identifying barriers: Creating solutions to improve family engagement. *School Community Journal, 26*(2), 161–184.

Baldwin, J. (1962). *The fire next time*. The Dial Press.

Ball, A. F. (2006). *Multicultural strategies for education and social change: Carriers of the torch in the United States and South Africa*. Teacher College Press.

Banks, C.A., & Banks, J.A. (1995). Equity pedagogy: An essential component of multicultural education. *Theory into Practice, 34*(3), 152-158.

Banks, J. A. (2019). *An introduction to multicultural education* (6th ed.). Pearson.

Baptist, E. E. (2014). *The half has never been told: Slavery and the making of American capitalism*. Basic Books.

Beck, M. & Malley, J. (2003, March). *A pedagogy of belonging*. The International Child and Youth Care Network. https://www.cyc-net.org/cyc-online/cycol-0303-belonging.html

Benito, M. (2018, February 27). *Katy ISD board votes to end dual language immersion program*. Khou.com. https://www.khou.com/article/news/education/katy-isd-board-votes-to-end-dual-language-immersion-program/285-523619544

Birch, S. H., & Ladd, G. W. (1997). The teacher-child relationship and children's early school adjustment. *Journal of School Psychology, 35*, 61–79.

Blanton, C. K. (2007). *The strange career of bilingual education in Texas, 1836-1981*. Texas A&M University Press.

Booker, K.C., & Lim, J.H. (2018). Belongingness and pedagogy: Engaging African American girls in middle school mathematics. *Youth and Society, 50*(8), 1037–1055.

Books, S. (2007). Devastation and disregard: Reflections on Katrina, child poverty, and educational opportunity. In S. Books (Ed.), *Invisible children in society and its schools*. (pp. 1–22). Lawrence Erlbaum.

Boonk, L., Gijselaers, H.J.M., Ritzen, H., & Brand-Gruewel, S. (2018). A review of the relationship between parental involvement indicators and academic achievement. *Educational Research Review, 24*, 10–30.

Bordalba, M. M., & Bochaca, J. G., (2019). Digital media for family-school communication? Parents' and teachers' beliefs, *Computers & Education, 132*, 44–62, https://doi.org/10.1016/j.compedu.2019.01.006.

Borich, G.D. (2015). Observation skills for effective teaching: Research based practices. 7th Ed. Boulder, CO: Paradigm Publishers.

Borrello, S. (2016, April 29). ABC News. *National teacher of the year tells students helping others is most important.* https://abcnews.go.com/US/national-teacher-year-tells-students-helping-important/story?id=38760931

Bowden, E. (2019, September 22). Florida 6-year-old arrested, handcuffed for elementary school tantrum. *New York Post.* https://nypost.com/2019/09/22/florida-6-year-old-arrested-handcuffed-for-elementary-school-tantrum/

Boykin, A. W., Coleman, S. T., Lilja, A. J., & Tyler, K. M. (2004). *Building on children's cultural assets in simulated classroom performance environments: Research vistas in the communal learning paradigm* (Report No. 68). Baltimore: Johns Hopkins University, Center for Research on the Education of Students Placed at Risk (CRESPAR).

Braden, E. G., & Rodriguez, S. C. (2016). Beyond mirrors and windows: A critical content analysis of Latinx children's books. *Journal of Language and Literacy Education, 12*(2), 56–83.

Bradley, J. (2021, January 7). *Resources for teachers on the days after the attack on the U.S. capitol.* beyond the stoplight. https://beyondthestoplight.com/2021/01/06/resources-for-teachers-on-the-days-after-the-attack-on-the-u-s-capitol/

Brandon, R. R. (2007). African American parents: Improving connections with their child's educational environment. *Intervention in School and Clinic, 43*(2), 116–120.

Brown, D. L. (2018, August 24). *Slavery's bitter roots: In 1619, '20 and odd Negroes' arrived in Virginia.* Washington Post. https://www.washingtonpost.com/news/retropolis/wp/2018/08/24/slaverys-bitter-roots-in-1619-20-and-odd-negroes-arrived-in-virginia/

Brown, H. D., & Lee, H. (2015). *Teaching by principles: An interactive approach to language pedagogy* (4th ed.). Pearson Education.

Brown, D. (1970). *Bury my heart at wounded knee.* Holt Paperbacks.

Buchanan, L.B. & Fox, S. G. (2019). On windows and mirrors in teacher education program materials: A content analysis of human demographics in one picture book collection. *Multicultural Perspectives, 21*(4), 189–201.

Burke, M. (2020, May 15). *Breonna Taylor police shooting: What we know about the Kentucky woman's death.* NBC News. https://www.nbcnews.com/news/us-news/breonna-taylor-police-shooting-what-we-know-about-kentucky-woman-n1207841

Burns, M. (2016, November 22). *5 strategies to deepen student collaboration*. Edutopia. https://www.edutopia.org/article/5-strategies-deepen-student-collaboration-mary-burns

Byrd, C. M. (2016). Does culturally relevant teaching work? An examination from student perspectives. *SAGE Open, 6*(3), 215824401666074. https://doi.org/10.1177/2158244016660744

Camera, L. (2021, June 23). Bills banning critical race theory advance in states despite its absence in many classrooms. *U.S. News*. https://www.usnews.com/news/education-news/articles/2021-06-23/bills-banning-critical-race-theory-advance-in-states-despite-its-absence-in-many-classrooms

Carlisle Indian School Project. (2020, June 17). Carlisle Indian School Project. https://carlisleindianschoolproject.com

Carter, D. J. (2008). Cultivating a critical race consciousness for African American school success. *Educational Foundations, 22*(1–2), 11–28.

Cartledge, G., Keesey, S., Bennett, J. G., Ramnath, R., & Council, M. R. III (2016). Culturally relevant literature: What matters most to primary-age urban learners. *Reading & Writing Quarterly, 32*(5), 399–426. https://doi.org/10.1080/10573569.2014.955225

Cassetta, G., & Sawyer, B. (2015). *Classroom management matters: The social-emotional learning approach children deserve*. Heinemann.

Collaborative for Academic, Social, and Emotional Learning. (n.d.). *What is SEL?* Author. https://casel.org/what-is-sel

Center for Disease Control. (2020, July 15). *Coronavirus disease 2019 (COVID-19)*. Centers for Disease Control and Prevention. https://www.cdc.gov/coronavirus/2019-ncov/prevent-getting-sick/social-distancing.html

Cohn-Vargas, B. (2015, May 29). Identity safe classrooms and schools. *Teaching Tolerance.* https://www.tolerance.org/magazine/identity-safe-classrooms-and-Schools

Cokley, K. O. (2014). *The myth of Black anti-intellectualism: A true psychology of African American students*. Praeger.

Communities for Just Schools Fund. (2020, May 12). *When SEL is used as another form of policing*. Medium. https://medium.com/@justschools/when-sel-is-used-as-another-form-of-policing-fa53cf85dce4

Cooper, C. W. (2009). Parent involvement, African American mothers, and the politics of educational care. *Equity & Excellence in Education*, 42(4), 379–394.

Costello, B., Wachtel, J., & Wachtel T. (2009). *The restorative practices handbook for teachers disciplinarians and administrators*. International Institute for Restorative Practices.

Cox, C. (2020, January 24). Texas teen banned from attending graduation after refusing to cut dreadlocks. *USAT Network.*

Daniels, K. F. (2019, October 6). *Georgia high school teacher investigated for telling class the Confederate flag is 'Like a white trash save the date card'*. The Root. https://www.theroot.com/georgia-high-school-teacher-investigated-for-telling-cl-1838824764?utm_source=theroot_facebook&utm_medium=socialflow

Darling-Hammond, L. (2010). *The flat world and education: How America's commitment to equity will determine our future.* Teachers College Press.

Davidson, J. (2017, July 26). *Restoring justice.* Teaching Tolerance. https://www.tolerance.org/magazine/summer-2014/restoring-justice

Davis, J., & Martin, D.B. (2018). Racism, assessment, and instructional practices: Implications for mathematics teachers of African American students. *Journal of Urban Mathematics Education, 11(1,2),* 45–68.

de Boer, H., Timmermans, A. C., & van der Werf, M. P. C. (2018). The effects of teacher expectation interventions on teachers' expectations and student achievement: Narrative review and meta-analysis, *Educational Research and Evaluation, (24)* 3–5, 180–200. http://doi.org/10.1080/13803611.2018.1550834

De La Rosa, S. (2019, November 27). *Report: Minority students overlooked in gifted identification process.* K–12 Dive. https://www.k12dive.com/news/report-minority-students-overlooked-in-gifted-identification-process/568154/

DeGruy, J. (2005). *Post traumatic slave syndrome: America's legacy of enduring injury and Healing.* Uptone Press.

Delisle, J. R. (2015, January 6). *Differentiation doesn't work.* Education Week. https://www.edweek.org/ew/articles/2015/01/07/differentiation-doesnt-work.html

Delpit, L. (2006). *Other people's Children: Cultural conflict in the classroom.* The New Press.

Derman-Sparks, L., ABC Task Force. (2012). *Ten quick ways to analyze children's books for sexism and racism.* Teaching for Change. https://www.teachingforchange.org/wp-content/uploads/2012/08/ec_tenquickways_english.pdf

Derman-Sparks, L. & Phillips, C.B. (1997). *Teaching/learning anti-racism: A developmental approach.* Teachers College Press.

Derman-Sparks, L. (1989). *Anti-bias curriculum: Tools for empowering young children.* National Association for the Education of Young People.

Dewey, J. (1897). My pedagogic creed. *School Journal, 54,* 77–80.

DiAngelo, R. (2018). *White fragility: Why it's so hard for white people to talk about racism.* Beacon Press.

Diemer, M. A, Marchand, A. D., McKellar, S. E., & Malanchuk, O. (2016). Promotive and corrosive factors in African American students' math beliefs and achievement. *J Youth Adolescence, 45,* 1208–1225.

Donahue-Keegan D., Villegas-Reimers E., & Cressey, J. M. (2019). Integrating social-emotional learning and culturally responsive teaching in teacher education preparation programs: The Massachusetts experience so far. *Teacher Education Quarterly, 46*(4), 150–168.

Douglass, F. (1968). *Narrative of the life of Frederick Douglass.* New American Library.

Dual Language Education of New Mexico. (2020, March 2). *What is dual language education?* Dual Language Education of New Mexico. https://www.dlenm.org/who-we-are/what-is-dual-language-education/

DuBois, W. E. B. (1994). *The souls of Black folk.* Gramercy Books.

Ebersole, M., Kanahele-Mossman, H., & Kawakami, A. (2016). Culturally responsive teaching: Examining teachers' understandings and perspectives. *Journal of Education and Training Studies, 4*(2), 97–104.

Ed Trust - West. (2020, April 15). *Education equity in crisis: The digital divide.* The Education Trust - West. https://west.edtrust.org/resource/education-equity-in-crisis-the-digital-divide

Eddo-Lodge, R. (2014, February 22). Why I'm no longer talking to white people about race. *Renieddolodge.* http://renieddolodge.co.uk/why-im-no-longer-talking-to-white-people-about-race

Education Commission of the States. (2012). Your education policy team. https://www.ecs.org/clearinghouse/01/05/51/10551.pdf

Emdin, C. (2016). *For white folks who teach in the hood...and the rest of ya'll too: Reality pedagogy and urban education.* Beacon Press.

Epstein, J. L. (2011). *School, family, and community partnerships: Preparing educators and Improving schools* (2nd ed.). Westview Press.

Ferlazzo, L. (2011). Involvement or engagement? *Educational leadership, 68*(8), 10–14.

Finley, A. M. (2018). Fostering belongingness pedagogy for English language learners. *BC TEAL Journal, 3*(1), 37–48.

Foner, E. (2000, April 9). *Was Abraham Lincoln a racist?* Los Angeles Times. https://www.latimes.com/archives/la-xpm-2000-apr-09-bk-17473-story.html

Fowler, S.(2017, March 14). *Can people really change?* HuffPost. https://www.huffpost.com/entry/can-people-really-change_b_58c7f13ae4b03400023f4b2b

Freire, P. (2000). *Pedagogy of the oppressed.* Continuum.

Friedman, Z. (2020, July 25). *Stimulus update: $600 a week unemployment benefits end today.* Forbes. https://www.forbes.com/sites/zackfriedman/2020/07/24/unemployment-benefits-end-tomorrow/#23a42bc749d6

Furey, W. (2020). The stubborn myth of "learning styles". *Education Next, 20*(3), 8–12. https://www.educationnext.org/stubborn-myth-learning-styles-state-teacher-license-prep-materials-debunked-theory/

Gatto, J. T. (2017). *Dumbing us down: The hidden curriculum of compulsory schooling.* New Society Publishers.

Gay, G. (2010). *Culturally responsive teaching: Theory, research, and practice* (2nd ed.). Teachers College Press.

Gay, G., & Kirkland, K. (2003). Developing cultural critical consciousness and self-reflection in pre-service teacher education. *Theory into Practice, 42*(3), 181–187.

George, G. (2017). *Restorative practices.* RPforSchools. http://rpforschools.net/pdfs/oZ8_RestorativeProcesses.pdf

Gibson, P. A., & Haight, W. (2013). Caregivers' moral narratives of their African American children's out-of-school suspensions: Implications for effective family-school collaborations. *Social Work, 58*(3), 263–272. https://doi.org/10.1093/sw/swt017

Gibson, V. (2020, July 22). *Working toward culturally responsive assessment practices.* NCTE. https://ncte.org/blog/2020/02/working-toward-culturally-responsive-assessment-practice/

Goldsmith, J. S., & Robinson Kurpius, S. E. (2018). Fostering the academic success of their children: Voices of Mexican immigrant parents. *The Journal of Educational Research, 111*(5), 564–573.

Gollygee [username] (2015, Jan 8). *From Tim Wise re free speech & anti-Muslim satire.* Democratic Underground. https://www.democraticunderground.com/10026058528

Gonzalez, N., Moll, L. C., & Amanti, K. (2005). *Funds of knowledge: Theorizing practices in households, communities, and classrooms.* Lawrence Erlbaum Associates.

Gooden, M. & Dantley, M. (2012). Centering race in a framework for leadership preparation. *Journal of Research on Leadership Education, 7,* 237–253. https://doi.org/10.1177/1942775112455266

Goodenow, C. (1993). Classroom belonging among early adolescent students: Relationships to motivation and achievement. Journal of Early Adolescence, 13(1), 21–43. https://doi.org/10.1177/0272431693013001002

Gordon-Reed, A. (2021). *On juneteenth.* Liveright Publishing Corporation.

Gorski, P. (2016a). Equity literacy: More than celebrating culture. *DiversityinEd.com.* https://08a3a74a-dec5-426e-8385-bdc09490d921.filesusr.com/ugd/38199c_6e253f01e770480ba3d34822277a538c.pdf

Gorski, P. (2016b). Rethinking the role of "culture" in educational equity: From cultural competence to equity literacy. *Multicultural Perspectives, 18*(4), 221–226.

Gorksi, P. (2019). Equity literacy for educators: Definition and abilities. *Equity Literacy Institute.* https://08a3a74a-dec5-426e-8385-bdc09490d921.filesusr.com/ugd/38199c_8d07da3e4cea48c1bcf21882694048ab.pdf

Gorski, P., & Swalwell, K. (2015). Equity literacy for all. *Educational Leadership, 72*(6), 34–40.

Greer, T. M., & Spalding, A. (2017). The role of age in understanding the psychological effects of racism for African Americans. *Cultural Diversity and Ethnic Minority Psychology, 23*(4), 588–594. https://doi.org/10.1037/cdp0000148

Grice, S. (2019/2020). *The conscious educator: Becoming culturally responsive teachers and schools.* Bookstand Publishing.

Grice, S. (2020). Perceptions of family engagement between African American families and schools: A Review of Literature. *Journal of Multicultural Affairs, (5)*2. https://scholarworks.sfasu.edu/jma/vol5/iss2/4

Grice, S. (2021). Content plus culture: Effective strategies for successful math teachers of Black girls. *The Lighthouse Almanac, 4*(1). http://bbamath.org/index.php/lighthouse/

Haberman, M. (1995). Selecting 'star teachers' for children and youth in urban poverty. *The Phi Delta Kappan, 76*(10), 777–782.

Halberstadt, A., & Shipman, M. (2020, July 6). *Future teachers more likely to view Black children as angry, even when they are not.* NC State News. https://news.ncsu.edu/2020/07/race-anger-bias-kids/

Hale-Benson, J. E., & Hilliard, A. G., III. (1986). *Black children: Their roots, culture, and learning.* Johns Hopkins University Press.

Haley, A. (1964). *The autobiography of Malcom X as told to Alex Haley.* Ballantine Books.

Hammond, Z. (2015). *Culturally responsive teaching and the brain.* Corwin.

Helibrun, A., Cornell, D., & Konold, T. (2018). Authoritative school climate and suspension rates in middle schools: Implications for reducing the racial disparity in school discipline. *Journal of School Violence, 17*(3). 324–338. https://doi.org./10.1080/15388220.2017.1368395

Henderson, A.T., & Mapp, K.L., (2002). *A new wave of evidence: Impact of school, family, and community connections on student achievement.* SEDL.

Hilaski, D. (2020). Addressing the mismatch through culturally responsive literacy instruction. *Journal of Early Childhood Literacy, 20*(2), 356–384. https://doi.org/10.1177/1468798418765304

Hill, E., Tiefenthäler, A., Triebert, C., Jordan, D., Willis, H., & Stein, R. (2020, May 31). *How George Floyd was killed in police custody*. The New York Times. https://www.nytimes.com/2020/05/31/us/george-floyd-investigation.html

Hill-Jackson, V., & Stafford, D. (2017). *Better teachers, better schools: What star teachers know, believe, and do*. Information Age.

Hirsch, C. (2020, April 14). *COVID-19 pandemic highlights lack of internet and technology access in rural school districts*. ABC17NEWS. https://abc17news.com/news/coronavirus/2020/04/14/covid-19-pandemic-highlights-lack-of-internet-and-technology-access-in-rural-school-districts/

Hobson, J., & Hagan, A. (2020, March 5). *What democratic socialism means in the U.S.* WBUR. https://www.wbur.org/hereandnow/2020/03/05/bernie-sanders-and-democratic-socialism

Hoffman, D. M. (2009). Reflecting on social emotional learning: A critical perspective on trends in the United States. Review of Educational Research, 79, 533–556. https://doi.org/10.3102/0034654308325184

Hoffman, S. (2014). Zero benefit: Estimating the effect of zero tolerance discipline policies on racial disparities in schools. *Educational Policy, 28*(1), 69–95.

Howard, G. R. (2016). *We can't teach what we don't know: White teachers, multiracial schools* (3rd ed.). Teachers College Press.

Hughes, J. N., Gleason, K. A., & Zhang, D. (2005). Relationship influences on teachers' perceptions of academic competence in academically at-risk minority and majority first grade students. *Journal of School Psychology, 43*, 303–320. https://doi.org/10.1016/j.jsp.2005.07.001

The Institute for Restorative Justice and Restorative Dialogue (2020, March 10). *Institute for Restorative Justice and Restorative Dialogue*. Author. https://irjrd.org

The International Institute for Restorative Practices (n.d.). *Home - IIRP Graduate School*. https://www.iirp.edu

Ishimaru, A. (2020). *Just schools: Building equitable collaborations with families and communities*. Teachers College Press.

Ishimaru, A. (2013). From heroes to organizers: Principals and education organizing in urban school reform. *Educational Administration Quarterly, 49*(1), 3–51. https://doi.org/10.1177/0013161X12448250

Iwai, Y. (2015) Using multicultural children's literature to teach diverse perspectives. *Kappa Delta Pi Record, 51*(2), 81–86. https://doi.org/10.1080/00228958.2015.1023142

Jackson, T. O., & Boutte, G. S. (2018). Exploring culturally relevant/responsive pedagogy as praxis in teacher education, *The New Educator, 14*(2), 87–90.

Jett, C.C. (2013). Culturally responsive collegiate mathematics education: Implications for African American students. *Interdisciplinary Journal of Teaching and Learning, 3*(2), 102–116.

Jeynes, W. H. (2013, February). Research digest: A meta-analysis of the efficacy of different types of parental involvement programs for urban students. *FINE Newsletter, 5*(1). https://archive.globalfrp.org/publications-resources/browse-our-publications/a-meta-analysis-of-the-efficacy-of-different-types-of-parental-involvement-Programs-for-urban-students

Johnson, D. W., & Johnson, R. T. (1999). Making cooperative learning work. *Theory Into Practice, 38*, 67–73.

Johnson, S. (2019). U.S. education and the persistence of slavery. *Journal of Curriculum and Pedagogy, 17*(1), 5–24. https://doi.org/10.1080/15505170.2019.1618757

Jones, R. (2021, January 7). *Opinion: This is what it looks like when toxic white privilege is left unchecked*. CNN. https://www.cnn.com/2021/01/07/opinions/capitol-rioters-contrast-with-june-2020-black-lives-matter-jones/index.html

Jupp, J. C., Leckie, A., Cabrera, N. L., & Utt, J. (2019) Race-evasive white teacher identity studies 1990–2015: What can we learn from 25 years of research? *Teachers College Record, 121*, 1–58.

Jussim, L., Eccles, J., & Madon, S. (1996). Social perception, social stereotypes, and teacher expectations: Accuracy and the quest for the powerful self-fulfilling prophecy. In M. P. Zanna (Ed.), Advances in experimental social psychology (Vol. 28, pp. 281–388). Academic Press. https://doi.org/10.1016/S0065-2601(08)60240-3

Kalyanpur, M., & Harry, B. (2012). *Cultural reciprocity in special education: Building family-professional relationships*. Paul H. Brookes.

Kaur, H. (2018, June 25). *Actually, the US has a long history of separating families*. CNN. https://www.cnn.com/2018/06/24/us/us-long-history-of-separating-families-trnd/index.html

Kendi, I. X. (2016). *Stamped from the beginning: The definitive history of racist ideas in America*. Nation Books.

Kendi, I. X. (2019). *How to be an antiracist*. One World.

Khalifa, M. A. (2018). *Culturally responsive school leadership*. Race and Education.

Kimball, M., Smith, N., & Quartz. (2013, October 28). *The myth of 'I'm bad at math'*. The Atlantic. https://www.theatlantic.com/education/archive/2013/10/the-myth-of-im-bad-at-math/280914

King, L. J. (2020). *Perspectives of Black histories in schools*. Information Age.

King, M. L. (1963). Letter from Birmingham jail. *The Atlantic Monthly, 212*(2), 78–88.

King, M. L. (1968). *Where do we go from here: Chaos or community?* Beacon Press.

Kirschner, P. A. (2017). Stop propagating the learning styles myth. *Computers & Education, 106*, 166–171. https://doi.org/10.1016/j.compedu.2016.12.006

Kirwan Institute for the Study of Race and Ethnicity. (2015). kirwaninstitute.osu.edu

Kochhar, R. (2020). (2020, August 26). *Unemployment rose higher in three months of COVID-19 than it did in two years of the Great Recession*. Pew Research Center. https://www.pewresearch.org/fact-tank/2020/06/11/unemployment-rose-higher-in-three-months-of-covid-19-than-it-did-in-two-years-of-the-great-recession

Koppelman, K. L. (2017). *Understanding human differences.* Pearson.

Koren, P. E., DeChillo, N., & Friesen, B. J. (1992). Measuring empowerment in families whose children have emotional disabilities: A brief questionnaire. *Rehabilitation Psychology, 37*(4), 305–321. https://doi.org/10.1037/0090-5550.37.4.305

Kunc, N. (1992). The need to belong: Rediscovering Maslow's hierarchy of needs. In R. Villa, J. Thousand, W. Stainback, and S. Stainback (Eds.), *Restructuring for caring and effective education: An Administrative Guide to Creating Heterogeneous Schools* (pp. 25–39). Paul Brookes.

Kunjufu, J. (2012). *There is nothing wrong with Black students.* African American Images.

Ladson-Billings, G. (1995). But that's just good teaching! The case for culturally relevant pedagogy. *Theory into Practice, 34*(3), 159–165. http://doi.org/10.1080/00405849509543675

Ladson-Billings, G. (2009). *The dreamkeepers: Successful teachers of African American children.* Jossey-Bass.

Lamboy, L., Taylor, A., & Thompson, W. (2020). Paternalistic aims and (mis) attributions of agency: What the over-punishment of Black girls in US classrooms teaches us about just school discipline. *Theory and Research in Education, 18*(1), 59-77. https://doi.org/10.1177%2F1477878520912510

Lasater, K. (2019). Developing authentic family-school partnerships in a rural high school: Results of a longitudinal action research study. *School Community Journal, 29*(2), 157–182.

Lascala, M. (2020, April 27). *These education companies offer free, at-home learning portals for parents of students.* Good Housekeeping.

Lattimore, K. (2017, July 17). *When Black hair violates the dress code.* NPR.org. https://www.npr.org/sections/ed/2017/07/17/534448313/when-black-hair-violates-the-dress-code

Latunde, Y. C. (2018). Expanding their opportunities to engage: A case of the African American parent council. *The Journal of Negro Education, 87*(3), 270–284.

Le, H., Janssen, J., & Wubbels, T. (2018). Collaborative learning practices: Teacher and student perceived obstacles to effective student collaboration, *Cambridge Journal of Education, (48)*1, 103–122. https://doi.org/10.1080/0305764X.2016.1259389

Lee, A., & Sidner, S. (2020, June 1). *99 years ago today, America was shaken by one of its deadliest acts of racial violence.* CNN. https://www.cnn.com/2020/06/01/us/tulsa-race-massacre-1921-99th-anniversary-trnd/index.html

Li, C., & Lalani, F. (2020, April 29). *The COVID-19 pandemic has changed education forever. This is how*. World Economic Forum. https://www.weforum.org/agenda/2020/04/coronavirus-education-global-covid19-online-digital-learning

Loewen, J. (2005). *Sundown towns. A hidden dimension of American racism*. The New Press.

Loewen, J. (2007). *Lies my teacher told me: Everything your American history textbook got wrong*. Touchstone.

Long, C. (2016, January 26). The far-reaching effects of implicit bias in the classroom. *NEAToday*. http://neatoday.org/2016/01/26/implicit-bias-in-the-classroom/

Lynch, M. (2020, May 9). *How teacher expectations influence student performance*. The Edvocate. https://www.theedadvocate.org/how-teacher-expectations-influence-student-performance/

Macedo, D., & Bartholome, L. (2000). *Dancing with bigotry: Beyond the politics of tolerance*. St. Martin's.

Madda, M. J. (2020, June 1). *Dena Simmons: Without context, social-emotional learning can backfire*. EdSurge. https://www.edsurge.com/news/2019-05-15-dena-simmons-without-context-social-emotional-learning-can-backfire

Maslow, A. (1970). *Motivation and Personality* (3rd ed.). Harper & Row Publishers.

McLaughlin, E. C. (2020, June 5). *Ahmaud Arbery was hit with a truck before he died, and his killer allegedly used a racial slur, investigator testifies.* CNN. https://www.cnn.com/2020/06/04/us/mcmichaels-hearing-ahmaud-arbery/index.html

Meador, D. (2019, July 5). *10 ways for teachers to build positive relationships with students.* ThoughtCo. https://www.thoughtco.com/develop-positive-relationships-with-students-3194339

Meltzer, M. (1971). *Slavery: From the rise of western civilization to today.* Dell Publishing Co.

Mendez, M. (2020, April 21). *A dream come true: African American studies course gets final approval to be offered across Texas.* Dallas News. https://www.dallasnews.com/news/politics/2020/04/17/a-dream-come-true-african-american-studies-course-gets-final-approval-to-be-offered-across-texas

Meraji, S. M. (2019, March 21). *50 years ago students shut down this college to demand ethnic studies courses.* NPR. https://www.npr.org/2019/03/21/705594577/50-years-ago-students-shut-down-this-college-to-demand-ethnic-studies-courses

Metta, J. (2016, July 10). *I, racist.* HuffPost. https://www.huffpost.com/entry/i-racist_b_7770652

Miami Herald Editorial Board. (2020, May 29). In Miami, too, white lies put black lives in danger. They're reprehensible-and racist. *Miami Herald.* https://www.miamiherald.com/opinion/editorials/article243060831.html

Miller, C. C. (2018, September 10) Does teacher diversity matter in student learning? *New York Times.* https://www.nytimes.com/2018/09/10/upshot/teacher-diversity-effect-students-learning.html

Miller, G. E., Lines, C., Sullivan, E., & Hermanutz, K. (2013). Preparing educators to partner with families. *Teaching Education, 24*(2), 150–163.

Milner, H. R., Cunningham. H. B., Delale-O'Connor, L., & Kestenberg, E. G. (2019). *These kids are out of control: Why we must reimagine classroom management for equity.* Corwin.

Minor, C. E. (2016). Racial differences in mathematics test scores for advanced mathematics students. *The High School Journal, 99,* 193–210.

Moll, L. C., Amanti, C., Neff, D., & Gonzalez, N. (1992). Funds of knowledge for teaching: Using a qualitative approach to connect homes and classrooms. *Theory Into Practice, 31*(2), 132–141.

Morris, M. W. (2016). *Pushout: The criminalization of Black girls in schools.* The New Press.

Morrison, L. (2019). "Watch your tone, fix your face, and other unspoken rules for educators of color." The Educator's Room. https://theeducatorsroom.com/opinionwatch-your-tone-fix-your-face-andother-Unspoken-rules-for-educators-ofcolor

Morton, C.H. (2014). A story of African American students as mathematics learners. *International Journal of Education in Mathematics, Science, and Technology, 2*(3), 234–245.

Mulholland, Q. (2015, May 14). *The case against standardized testing*. Harvard Political Review. https://harvardpolitics.com/united-states/case-standardized-testing

National Assessment of Educational Progress. (2019). *NAEP report card: Reading grade 4*. Author. https://www.nationsreportcard.gov/reading/?grade=4

National Association for Multicultural Education. (n.d.). *What is equity? - NAME learn*. National Association for Multicultural Education. https://www.nameorg.org/learn/what_is_equity.php

National Center for Education Statistics. (2017a). *2017 reading state snapshot report: California, grade 4, public schools*. The nation's report card. https://nces.ed.gov/nationsreportcard/subject/publications/stt2017/pdf/2018039CA4.pdf

National Center for Education Statistics. (2017b). *Status and trends in the education of racial and ethnic groups 2017*. https://nces.ed.gov/pubs2017/2017051.pdf

National Center for Education Statistics. (2019). *Spotlight A: Characteristics of Public School Teachers by Race/Ethnicity*. Status and Trends in the Education of Racial and Ethnic Groups. https://nces.ed.gov/programs/raceindicators/spotlight_a.asp#:~:text=The%20percentage%20of%20minority5,minority%20students%20(10%20percent)%2C

New York State Education Department. (2019). *Culturally responsive-sustaining education framework*. New York State Education Department. http://www.nysed.gov/crs/framework

Netflix. (2020, March 26). *#blackAF* [Video]. YouTube. https://www.youtube.com/watch?v=O-LtbHykms0

Nieto, S. (2010). *Language, culture, and teaching: A critical perspective*. Routledge.

Norris, K. E. L. (2018). Effective parent partnerships between schools and diverse families. In K. E. L. Norris & S. Collier (Eds.), *Social Justice and Parent Partnerships in Multicultural Education Contexts* (pp. 1–17). IGI Global.

Norton, M. I., & Sommers, S. R. (2011). Whites see racism as a zero-sum game that they are now losing. *Perspectives on Psychological Science, 6*(3), 215–218. https://doi.org/10.1177/1745691611406922

Ortega, L., Lyubansky, M., Nettles, S., & Espelage, D. L. (2016). Outcomes of a restorative circles program in a high-school setting. *Psychology of Violence, 6*(3), 459–468.

Ortiz, Paul. (2018). *An African American and Latin history of the United States*. Beacon Press.

Owens, J., & McLanahan, S. S. (2019). Unpacking the drivers of racial disparities, in school suspension and expulsion. *Social Forces, 98*(4), 1548–1577. https://doi.org/10.1093/sf/soz095

Park Dahlen, S., & Huyck, D. (2019, June 19). *Picture this: Diversity in children's books 2018 infographic*. sarahpark.com blog. https://readingspark.wordpress.com/2019/06/19/picture-this-diversity-in-childrens-books-2018-infographic

Parker, L., & Lynn, M. (2002). What's race got to do with it? Critical race theory's conflicts with and connections to qualitative research methodology and epistemology. *Qualitative Inquiry, 8*(1), 7–22.

Pathak, A., & Intratat, C. (2012). Use of semi-structured interviews to investigate teacher perceptions of student collaboration. *Malaysian Journal of ELT Research, 8*(1), 1–10.

Pearson, J. N., Akamoglu, Y., Chung, M., & Meadan, H. (2019). Building family-professional partnerships with culturally, linguistically, and economically diverse families of young children. *Multicultural Perspectives, 21*(4), 208–216.

Peck, C., & Reitzug, U.C. (2018). Discount stores, discount(ed) community? Parent and family engagement, community outreach, and urban turnaround school. *Education and Urban Society, 50*(8), 675–696.

Positive Psychology Program. (2018, May 2). *Self-fulfilling prophecy in psychology: 10 examples and definition.* PositivePsychology.com. https://positivepsychologyprogram.com/self-fulfilling-prophecy

Powell, T. & Coles, J. A. (2021). 'We still here': Black mothers' personal narratives of sense making and resisting antiblackness and the suspensions of their Black children. *Race Ethnicity and Education, 24*(1), 76–95. https://doi.org/10.1080/13613324.2020.1718076

Pritchard, A. (2013). *Ways of learning: Learning theories and learning styles in the classroom* (3rd ed.). Taylor and Francis.

Project Implicit. (n.d.). *Implicit association test.* Project Implicit. https://implicit.harvard.edu/implicit/takeatest.html

Raffaele Mendez, L. M., & Knoff, H. M. (2003). Who gets suspended from school and why: A demographic analysis of schools and disciplinary infractions in a large school district. *Education and Treatment of Children,* 26(1), 30–51.

Ranseth, J. (2017, August 24). *Gandhi didn't actually say "Be the change you want to see in the world." Here's the real quote.* https://josephranseth.com/gandhi-didnt-say-be-the-change-you-want-to-see-in-the-world

Ratcliffe, S. (2017). *Oxford essential quotations* (5th ed.). Oxford University Press. https://www.oxfordreference.com/view/10.1093/acref/9780191843730.001.0001/acref-9780191843730

Reading Is Fundamental. (2015). *Mirrors, windows, and sliding glass doors.* www.rif.org.

Reynolds, J. & Kendi, I. X. (2020). *Stamped: Racism, antiracism, and you.* Little, Brown and Company.

Rosenberg, E. (2018, November 3). The schoolteachers who dressed up as 'Mexicans' and a MAGA wall for Halloween have been suspended. *The Washington Post.* https://www.washingtonpost.com/nation/2018/11/03/these-school-teachers-dressed-up-mexicans-wall-halloween-it-didnt-go-well

Rosenthal, R., & Jacobson, L. (1968). *Pygmalion in the classroom: Teacher expectations and pupils' intellectual development.* Holt, Rinehart and Winston.

Rubie-Davies, C. (2015, June 23). *The teacher expectation project*. Society for Personality and Social Psychology. https://spsp.org/news-center/blog/the-teacher-expectation-project

Rubie-Davies, C. M. (2018). *Teacher Expectations in Education*. Routledge.

Ruiz-Grossman, S. (2019, May 17). *Black girls detail harsh consequences of being seen as older than white peers*. HuffPost. https://www.huffpost.com/entry/black-girls-adultification-white-report_n_5cdf3a51e4b09e057803fbe9

Salkind, N. J. (2008). Learning style. *Encyclopedia of educational psychology*. Sage.

Santhanam, L. (2019, October 18). *Youth suicide rates are on the rise in the U.S*. PBS NewsHour. https://www.pbs.org/newshour/health/youth-suicide-rates-are-on-the-rise-in-the-u-s

Salter, P. S., Adams, G., & Perez, M. J. (2018). Racism in the structure of everyday worlds: A cultural-psychological perspective. *Current Directions in Psychological Science, 27*(3), 150–155. https://doi.org/10.1177/0963721417724239

San Francisco Unified School District. (2010) Restorative practices: Curriculum and supporting documents. http://www.healthiersf.org/RestorativePractices/Resources/index.php

Serwer, A. (2019, December 23). *The fight over the 1619 project is not about the facts*. The Atlantic. https://www.theatlantic.com/ideas/archive/2019/12/historians-clash-1619-project/604093

Shaw, G., & Wierenga, A. (2002). *Restorative practices/community conferencing pilot evaluation*. University of Melbourne.

Sheldon, S. B., & Epstein, J. L. (2002). Improving student behavior and school discipline with family and community involvement. *Education and Urban Society, 35*(1), 4–26.

Simmons, D. (2019, April 19). *Why we can't afford whitewashed social-emotional learning.* ASCD. http://www.ascd.org/publications/newsletters/education_update/apr19/vol61/num04/Why_We_Can't_Afford_Whitewashed_Social-Emotional_Learning.aspx

Sims Bishop, R. (1990). Mirrors, windows, and sliding glass doors. Perspectives, 1(3), ix–xi.

Skiba, R. J., & Rausch, M. K. (2006). Zero tolerance, suspension, and expulsion: Questions of equity and effectiveness. In C. M. Evertson & C. S. Weinstein (Eds.), *Handbook of classroom management: Research, practice, and contemporary issues* (pp.1063–1089). Lawrence Erlbaum.

Slaten, C. D., Yough, M. S., Shemwell, D., Scalise, D. A., Elison, Z. M., & Hughes, H. (2014). "Eat. Sleep. Breathe. Study": Understanding what it means to belong at a university from the student perspective. *Excellence in Higher Education, 5*, 1–5. https://doi.org/10.5195/ehe.2014.117

Slattery, P. (2013). *Curriculum development in the postmodern era* (3rd ed.). Routledge.

Slavin, R. E. (2014). *Making cooperative learning powerful.* ASCD: Professional Learning & Community for Educators. https://www.ascd.org/publications/educational-leadership/oct14/vol72/num02/Making-Cooperative-Learning-Powerful.aspx

Sleeter, C. E. (2012). Confronting the Marginalization of Culturally Responsive Pedagogy. *Urban Education, 47*(3), 562–584. https://doi.org/10.1177/0042085911431472

Smith, C. (2019, August 24). *Texas board of education approves a Mexican-American studies course (but they won't call it that)*. Dallas News. https://www.dallasnews.com/news/education/2018/04/11/texas-board-of-education-approves-a-mexican-american-studies-course-but-they-won-t-call-it-that

Smith, P. (2020). "Mr. Wang doesn't really care how we speak!": Responsiveness in the practice of an exemplary Asian-American teacher. *Urban Review, 52*, 351–375. https://doi-org.srv-proxy2.library.tamu.edu/10.1007/s11256-019-00531-4

Smith, T. E., Sheridan, S. M., Kim, E. M., Park, S.; & Beretvas, S. N. (2020). The effects of family-school partnership interventions on academic and social-emotional functioning: A meta-analysis exploring what works for whom. *Educational Psychology Review, 32*, 511–544.

Solomon, D. (2020, March 19). *The coronavirus pandemic and the racial wealth gap*. Center for American Progress. https://www.americanprogress.org/issues/race/news/2020/03/19/481962/coronavirus-pandemic-racial-wealth-gap

Sparks, S. (2020, December 23). *Differentiated instruction: A primer*. Education Week. https://www.edweek.org/ew/articles/2015/01/28/differentiated-instruction-a-primer.html

Steele, C. M. (1995). Stereotype threat and the intellectual test performance of African Americans. *Journal of Personality and Social Psychology, 69*(5), 797–811.

Style, E. (1996). *Curriculum as a window or mirror.* The National SEED Project. From: www.nationalseedproject.org

Takaki, R. (2008). *A different mirror: A history of multicultural America.* Bay Back Books.

Takaki, R. (1998). *Strangers from a different shore.* Little, Brown and Company.

Tamura, E. (1993). *Americanization, acculturation, and ethnic identity: The Nisei generation in Hawaii.* University of Illinois Press.

Tatum, B. D. (1997). *Why are all the black kids sitting together in the cafeteria? And other conversations about race.* Basic Books.

Taylor, K. R. (2020, May 20). *Choosing restorative justice: Engagement, rather than punishment, fosters community and respect in the library.* School Library Journal. https://www.slj.com/?detailStory=Choosing-Restorative-Justice-Strategic-Engagement-not-Punishment-Fosters-Community-and-Respect-in-Library

Tenenbaum. H. R., & Ruck, M. D. (2007). Are teachers' expectations different for racial minority than for European American students? A meta-analysis. *Journal of Educational Psychology, 99*, 253–273. https://doi.org/10.1037/0022-0663.99.2.253

The Derek Bok Center for Teaching and Learning (n.d.). *Inclusive course design.* Derek Bok Center, Harvard University. https://bokcenter.harvard.edu/inclusive-course-design

The Schott Foundation (2018, August 2). *Restorative practices: Fostering healthy relationships & promoting positive discipline in schools*. Schott Foundation for Public Education. https://schottfoundation.org/resources/restorative-practices-toolkit

Thirteen. (2004). *Slavery and the making of America: Timeline*. PBS. Thirteen/WNET New York. https://www.thirteen.org/wnet/slavery/timeline/1676.html

Timmermans, A. C., Kuyper, H., & Van der Werf, G. (2015). Accurate, inaccurate or biased teacher expectations: Do Dutch teachers differ in their expectations at the end of primary education? *British Journal of Educational Psychology, 85*, 459–478. https://doi.org/10.1111/bjep.12087

Tomlinson, C. A. (2015, January 27). *Differentiation does, in fact, work*. Education Week. https://www.edweek.org/ew/articles/2015/01/28/differentiation-does-in-fact-work.html

Torres, C. (2019, February 19). *Unheard voices: Recentering discussions in the classroom* [Opinion]. Education Week. https://blogs.edweek.org/teachers/intersection-culture-and-race-in-education/2019/02/unheard_voices_re-centering_discussions_in_the_clawssroom.html

Tran, N., & Birman, D. (2017). Acculturation and assimilation: A qualitative inquiry of teacher expectations for Somali Bantu refugee students. *Education and Urban Society, 51*(2), 1–25. https://doi.org/10.1177/0013124517747033

Tschida, C., Ryan, C. L., & Swenson Ticknor, A. (2014). Building on windows and mirrors: Encouraging the disruption of single stories through children's literature. *Journal of Children's Literature, 40*(1), 28–39.

Tyack, D. B. (1984). *The one best system: A history of American urban education.* Harvard University Press.

USAGOV. (2020, August 26). *Government response to coronavirus, COVID-19.* Official Guide to Government Information and Services. https://www.usa.gov/coronavirus

U.S. Department of Education, National Center for Education Statistics. (1998). *Violence and discipline problems in U.S. public schools: 1996–97.* Author. https://nces.ed.gov/pubs98/98030.pdf

Valencia, R. (2010). *Dismantling contemporary deficit thinking: educational thought and practice.* Routledge.

Vera, A., & Ly, L. (2020, May 26). *White woman who called police on a Black man bird-watching in Central Park has been fired.* CNN. https://www.cnn.com/2020/05/26/us/central-park-video-dog-video-african-american-trnd/index.html

Villa, R. A. (2011, March 21). *What can collaboration with students look like?* SEEN Magazine. https://www.seenmagazine.us/Articles/Article-Detail/articleid/1301/what-can-collaboration-with-students-look-like

Villegas, A. M., & Lucas, T. (2002). Preparing Culturally Responsive Teachers: Rethinking the Curriculum. *Journal of Teacher Education*, 53(1), 20–32. https://doi.org/10.1177/0022487102053001003

Waters, L. (2020, January 2). *DeVos is stripping away civil rights protections for students with special needs*. Education Post. https://educationpost.org/devos-is-stripping-away-civil-rights-protections-for-students-with-special-needs

Weissberg, R. (2016, February 15). *Why social and emotional learning is essential for students*. Edutopia. https://www.edutopia.org/blog/why-sel-essential-for-students-weissberg-durlak-domitrovich-gullotta

Wendlandt, C. (2020, March 13). *A list of Houston school closures*. Houstonia Magazine. https://www.houstoniamag.com/news-and-city-life/houston-school-closures-list

Whan Choi, Y. (2020, March 31). *How to address racial bias in standardized testing*. Next Generation Learning Challenges. https://www.nextgenlearning.org/articles/racial-bias-standardized-testing

Will, M. (2020, November 19a). *Still mostly white and female: New federal data on the teaching profession*. Education Week. https://www.edweek.org/leadership/still-mostly-white-and-female-new-federal-data-on-the-teaching-profession/2020/04

Will, M. (2020, June 9b). *Teachers are as racially biased as everybody else, study shows*. Education Week. https://www.edweek.org/ew/articles/2020/06/09/teachers-have-racial-biases-too-study-shows.html

Williams, J. A. III, & Tehia, S. G. (2019). Teacher education and multicultural courses in North Carolina. *Journal for Multicultural Education, 13*(2), 155–168. https://doi.org/10.1108/JME-05-2018-0028

Williams, J. A., III, Persky, F. D., & Johnson, J. N. (2018). Does Longevity Matter? Teacher Experience and the Suspension of Black Middle School. *Journal of Urban Learning, Teaching, and Research, 14*, 50–62.

Wilson, M., & Yull, D. (2018). Keeping Black children pushed into, not out of, classrooms: Developing a race-conscious parent engagement project. *Journal of Black Psychology, 44*(2), 162–188.

Wise, T. (2017). *To those who say tearing down confederate statues erases history not the statues*. Facebook. https://www.facebook.com/timjacobwise/posts/to-those-who-say-tearing-down-confederate-statues-erases-history-nothe-statues-d/10154732123290969

Woodard, C. (2019, August 7). *6 strategies for building better student relationships*. Edutopia. https://www.edutopia.org/article/6-strategies-building-better-student-relationships

Woodson, C. G. (1933). *The mis-education of the Negro*. Associated Publishers.

Yamauchi, L. A., Ponte, E., Ratliffe, K. T., & Traynor, K. (2017). Theoretical and conceptual frameworks used in research on family-school partnerships. *School Community Journal, 27*(2), 9–34.

Ye Hee Lee, M. (2015, July 7). Yes, U.S. locks people up at a higher rate than any other country. *Washington Post.* https://www.washingtonpost.com/news/fact-checker/wp/2015/07/07/yes-u-s-locks-people-up-at-a-higher-rate-than-any-other-country

Yeung, B. (2008). Learning zone: Harlem project gives poor students an edge. *Edutopia.* https://www.edutopia.org/paul-tough-harlem-childrens-zone

Yolen, J. (1996). *Encounter.* Voyager Books.

Yosso, T. J. (2005). Whose culture has capital? A critical race theory discussion of community cultural wealth. *Race Ethnicity and Education, 8*(1), 69–91.

Young, Y. (2016). Teachers' implicit bias against black students starts in preschool, study finds. *The Guardian.* https://www.theguardian.com/world/2016/oct/04/black-students-teachers-implicit-racial-bias-preschool-study?CMP=share_btn_fb

YouTube Movies. (2012, October 15). Waiting for Superman [Video]. YouTube. https://www.youtube.com/watch?v=p2SZE8IA9RA

Zhou, G. & Zhang, Z. (2014). A study of the first-year international students at a Canadian university: Challenges and experiences with social integration. *Canadian and International Education, 43*(2). https://ir.lib.uwo.ca/cie-eci/vol43/iss2/7

Zinn, H. (2003). *A people's history of the United States*. HarperCollins.

Zinn, H., & Stefoff, R. (2009). *A young people's history of the United States*. Seven Stories Press.

www.ingramcontent.com/pod-product-compliance
Lightning Source LLC
LaVergne TN
LVHW012106070526
838202LV00056B/5645